Inner Worlds
of Meditation

Books by John-Roger

The Tao of Spirit
Forgiveness: The Key to the Kingdom
The Christ Within & The Disciples of Christ
   with the Cosmic Christ Calendar
Dream Voyages
Walking with the Lord
God Is Your Partner
Q&A from the Heart
Passage Into Spirit
Relationships—The Art of Making Life Work
Loving—Each Day
Wealth & Higher Consciousness
The Power Within You
The Spiritual Promise
The Spiritual Family
The Sound Current
The Signs of the Times
The Way Out Book
Sex, Spirit & You
Possessions, Projections & Entities
The Path to Mastership
Music is the Message
The Master Chohans of the Color Rays
Manual on Using the Light
The Journey of a Soul
Dynamics of the Lower Self
Drugs
The Consciousness of Soul
Buddha Consciousness
Blessings of Light
Baraka
Awakening Into Light

For further information, please contact:
Mandeville Press®
P.O. Box 513935
Los Angeles, CA 90051-1935
(213) 737-4055

Inner Worlds of Meditation

Revised Edition

John-Roger

Mandeville Press
Los Angeles, California

M

Mandeville Press
P.O. Box 513935
Los Angeles, CA 90051-1935

Printed in the United States of America

Library of Congress Catalog Card Number: 76-56625

I.S.B.N. 0-914829-45-9

For the Traveler teaches
the inner kingdom;
It teaches the inner realms
of consciousness;
It teaches the absoluteness
and purity of
each individual in the Soul
and shares with you
this nectar of life.

CONTENTS

PREFACE

The meditation techniques in this book have been taught by John-Roger in seminars all over the world. They have been developed as keys to Soul Transcendence, the process of becoming more aware of yourself as a Soul and, more than that, as one with God. These meditations work with the spiritual focus of the Light, and are designed for your upliftment. It is important that you do the meditations as described, with an understanding of the purpose and intent of each one. In order to understand the concepts that form a foundation for each meditation, we recommend that you read the introductory material in Chapter 1 completely before beginning any of the meditations. Then read each chapter fully before doing the technique it explains.

1

Introduction to Meditation & Spiritual Exercises

Your job is to awaken to the levels inside
of you that are asleep, to awaken to the
consciousness of love, Light, and Sound.

A growing trend toward meditation has been taking place. A great deal of information and many different forms and techniques of meditation are available through books, workshops, and meditation centers. Meditation has been used for many purposes—from calming and healing physical, emotional, and mental stress to experiencing higher levels of consciousness and achieving self-realization. Most meditative techniques are a passive process where you sit and try to still your body and empty your mind and consciousness of all thought and feeling. In reality, that is next to impossible to do. Thoughts and emotions are nearly always present in the human consciousness to some degree and will continually bypass almost any attempt to block them out or quiet them completely.

1

This type of passive meditation works up to a certain point. You can sit for twenty minutes or for hours, and you might gain some relaxation of your mind, emotions and physical body. You may sense more calm and quiet inside simply by removing yourself from a lot of outer stimulation and demands. But you can sit with a good book, focusing on what you are reading, and have the same experience. I get some of my best ideas when I'm reading, but it's not necessarily because of the book. As I focus on what I am reading, the scatter of my mind and resulting emotional chaos quiet down and I can tap into my own inner wisdom.

People often sit and meditate for long periods of time; they tap into their own emotional, astral or etheric bodies, into their own thought forms, into their own confusions and dilemmas, or into the "garbage" they pick up from other people. Meditation then becomes a self-defeating process.

I teach another dimension to the meditative process, which changes it from a passive technique of *emptying* the mind to an active technique of *directing* the mind and emotions. I call these active meditations "spiritual exercises," which suggests the activity of exercise combined with a spiritual focus and thrust. This book deals with spiritual exercises although I'll use the word meditation because it is familiar and many people are comfortable with it. When I say meditation, however, I am referring to the active process of spiritual exercises more than the passive process of emptying the mind.

The Soul is an extremely dynamic, forceful, creative unit of energy. It is *alive* in the truest, most pure sense of the word. It is the part of every person that never dies, always exists, always is. It is an extension of God and a spark of the Divine. It is your truest reality. The body, mind, and emotions are the vehicles through which your Soul gains experience in this world. They are not who you are. They are illusionary and transient.

Because the Soul is active and dynamically alive, you must become active and alive in order to know that essence of yourself. You must awaken yourself to that reality, that dynamic beingness that is your Soul. You cannot awaken to that which is active by being passive. You must become active to reach Soul consciousness. That is why I teach the active process of spiritual exercises as the key to Soul Transcendence.

In all of the spiritual exercise techniques, it is always best to combine the technique with the positive power of the Light. The Light is a pure energy from the high realms of God. It is the force that activates everything. It is the essence of the Holy Spirit. If you want success, it is essential that you ask for the power of the Light to work with you for the highest good during your meditation. That is your insurance that your meditation will be for your upliftment and your spiritual unfoldment.

The energies that are present during spiritual exercises, though they may seem subtle, are active and very powerful. Used in negativity, they can bring you great confusion and turmoil—and potentially, they could be destructive. Used in the Light they are an incredibly accelerated way to spiritual enlightenment. How you use them is up to you. If you have your own best interests at heart, you will begin every meditation with a prayer asking that the Light surround you, protect you, and fill you, that any negativity that may be released be cleared and dispersed into the Light, and that all that takes place during the meditation be for the highest good. When you ask for this in purity, sincerity and love, you are protected and your meditation will be a positive one for your upliftment and progression. If you feel an attunement with the Mystical Traveler, a spiritual consciousness that exists throughout all levels of God's creation, you may also ask for that consciousness to be with you and to work with you for the highest good. The Traveler resides in each one of us; it is a part that you may or may not be aware of. The Traveler is a guide into the higher levels of Spirit, the greater reality of God. This consciousness works with you in love, on the inner levels, and is available to you simply by asking.[1]

Preparing for Spiritual Exercises

As you move into meditation, create an environment that will enhance your meditation. You will need a time and space where you will not be disturbed. You might hang a "Please do not disturb" sign on your door, take the phone off the hook or turn on your answering machine with the volume off. Turn off the alarm on your watch if you have one. If you're thirsty, drink some water. If your stomach is growling, get a little something to eat. Have a blanket available if you need one. In other words, anticipate

---

[1] For more information about the Mystical Traveler, see the bibliography and "Books & Tapes by John-Roger" listing at the end of the book.

4

any possible distractions to your meditation and take care of them before you start.

Find a comfortable chair—but not so comfortable that you fall asleep. Wear comfortable clothing that won't make you fidget. Before you sit down, take a few minutes to stretch and breathe deeply. This can help release tension from the body, mind and emotions. Then sit quietly for a few minutes and let your body relax. As you relax, notice energy flowing freely through your body. Make it a point to let nothing that happens in the physical environment disturb you. You can do this by simply telling yourself that any noise you hear will help you to relax more deeply and lift higher in your consciousness. If somebody honks their car horn, be aware that it happened, but not disturbed by it. If the phone rings in the apartment next door, identify it as their phone and know that there is nothing you have to do about it. Use these things to lift you higher into your meditation. Use everything that happens as a tool for your own evolvement.

In spiritual exercises, you use a focal point through which to direct the energy of Spirit, the energy of Light. This focal point may be as organic as your own process of breathing, or it may involve an outside object, such as water or flame, or it may be a sound or mantra that you repeat or chant either outwardly (out loud) or inwardly (in silence). Some spiritual exercises have been developed to affect or work with specific areas of consciousness, but all spiritual exercises share the common purpose of lifting you into higher, more subtle, refined states of awareness and perception until you break through the illusions of this world into the consciousness of the Soul.

As you work with the meditations in this book, you may find that you are working with higher energies than usual. You may feel their intensity and their force in several ways. You may feel very warm as the spiritual energy comes in; it can increase circulation and cause the sensation of warmth. You may feel a tingling in your hands or feet or head, like small electrical charges. You may notice that your vision shifts or blurs. After doing the exercises, you may find it difficult to see physically. These techniques are designed to shift your awareness into higher dimensions, so don't be surprised by changes. Things come "back to normal" soon enough. Later in this chapter, I will describe some techniques for grounding yourself after meditation so that you can go about your daily life in a centered way.

While you are meditating, you may see colors either inwardly in the inner eye or outwardly. These may be the colors of your own aura being reflected to you. Or they might indicate the presence of a spiritual master. If you see the color purple, it may mean that the Mystical Traveler Consciousness is present with you, assisting you in releasing things from your consciousness that you no longer need and balancing past actions, otherwise known as karma. There's nothing for you to do except recognize that this is happening.

As you meditate, you may feel as though your body is changing shape or size. Your body might feel as though it has become huge, as though it fills the entire room. Or you might feel as though you're getting smaller and smaller. If you have your eyes open, things around you might look as though they are shrinking. These shifts indicate that your consciousness is moving within you, out of the confines of the body's boundaries into greater freedom. Don't let these sensations frighten you. They're all steps in your progression into the higher realms of Spirit.

As you bring spiritual frequencies into your body, this pure energy usually pushes out the negativity that you have held in your consciousness. So in the midst of meditation you may find yourself thinking ugly, destructive, angry words. Or you may feel your emotions well up inside of you and with them, great turmoil and distress. Or you may see disturbing images. These are often thoughts, feelings or images that you have blocked or suppressed into the lower levels of your consciousness, and they can surface as you meditate. The Light pushes them out and fills the space that they were taking in your consciousness. Don't be concerned. Don't try to make these things stop. Just let the words come up. Let the emotions come up. Let the pictures come up. Cry if you want to. It's your opportunity to clear yourself and move one step closer to your spiritual reality. As you move toward Soul consciousness, you will be confronting and clearing the negativity in your consciousness with the assistance of the Light. So if imbalances come up, you can just look at them, admit that they're there, bless them with the Light, forgive yourself, and let them go. They can be dispersed into the Light, and you can be clear of them. That's freedom.

When you are involved in practicing spiritual exercises, you are bringing your consciousness into an alert state and tapping into very dynamic forces. Some people find that if they do spiritual exercises late at night, they have a hard time getting to sleep afterwards. They attune to spiritual energy that brings them so wide awake they just can't turn the energy off. For other people, spiritual exercises seem to be a foolproof way to get to sleep. They do spiritual exercises for thirty minutes or so and then drop right off to sleep. Experiment and see which way it goes for you. It is very individual. You might find that some of the techniques bring you wide awake and others help you get to sleep. I want you to be aware of both possibilities. If certain exercises do keep you awake, you might want to schedule them during the day or early in the evening. The ones where you tend to drop off to sleep are naturally best done when you are ready for sleep.

Grounding Yourself After Spiritual Exercises

When you do a meditation where your con-sciousness moves within you and you feel things shift somewhere, somehow, or even that you step free of the body to some degree, you may find it difficult to come back to earth and readjust to the physical energies. There are a couple of good tech-niques that can help you bring all of your conscious-ness back into alignment and focus in this physical world. The first is simply to drink some water and stretch your body a little bit. Another technique is to say, inwardly or outwardly, the sound "E", as in "see." Starting with your voice very low, you say a long, sustained "eeeeeeeeeeeee," taking your voice from a low key up as high as you can, and then back down low again. As you do this, imagine the sound starting at your feet, moving up through your body to a point about a foot above your head at the highest tone, then back down to your feet as you go back down to the low tone. You can stand up as you do this, gently reaching for your toes as you start saying the "eeee" in the low tone, then gradually reaching up to above your head at the high tone, and back down to your toes as you go down to the low tone. It only takes a couple of seconds. Repeat it a few times, and you may be surprised at how back together you feel, balanced, centered, and ready to move on with your day.

Keeping a Journal

As you practice these spiritual exercises, you may want to keep track of which exercise you do, how long you do it, and any experiences you have during and after the exercise. For example, you might record that you did the flame meditation for 5 minutes on Monday. You might note that you saw a soft halo around the flame as you gazed, and that you stopped the meditation when you felt as though you were falling asleep, rather than focusing your energy out into the flame. You might note that you saw a spot of color in your inner vision as you sat quietly completing the meditation, and that the spot of color changed several times. Other than that, you might not have any other experience to report. However, the next morning, you might add that your dreams were extremely vivid, and that you remembered them in more detail than is usual for you. These are just some possibilities from one meditation.

Notice that you want to keep track of not only what meditation you did, but how long you did it and also anything you notice both during and after the meditation that seems different than usual for you, and therefore possibly a result of the meditation.

You might find some very beautiful poetic thoughts and feelings flowing through your consciousness. As you do these spiritual exercises, you are attuning yourself to the higher frequencies of Light, and your thoughts and feelings may be reflections of this attunement. Writing these things in your journal creates a beautiful record for you of your progress, and is also an inspiration to read when you need a boost.

I suggest that you get something that appeals to you to use as your journal, and use it only for this purpose. Some people buy beautiful journals and even a special pen, and keep them where they do their spiritual exercises. Other people like to use a 3-ring binder full of lined paper where they can track things under different subject headings, and add more paper as they need it. Others prefer a simple spiral bound notebook. Some people also keep a small tape recorder with them to record thoughts and awarenesses as they come up. You may find that your consciousness reveals awarenesses to you while you are driving or waiting for an appointment or at some other time when you don't have your journal with you. A tape recorder comes in very handy in this type of situation.

Be a scientist when it comes to checking out these spiritual exercises. You might want to track what you do by date. Or you might have a section for each meditation plus a general section to record your awarenesses and thoughts about the process of doing spiritual exercises. How you record your experiences is as individual as the experiences you have on your inner journey. Find what appeals to you; find the way that works for you, and use it.

⊕ ⊕ ⊕

A final note before moving into the exercises: it is extremely important that you do not teach these spiritual exercises to other people. If you would like to share these meditations with others, give them this book. Then they are responsible for reading all the information as it is presented here. If you teach these exercises to others, then you are responsible for giving all the information to them accurately. If you leave out something that causes them to fail, their failure comes back to you as the creator—and you must handle that, whether you want to or not. If you don't have total understanding and the ability to see what is happening within the consciousness of another, if you don't have the awareness to perceive the process of spiritual exercises and the past actions that are being balanced, then it is best (by far!) not to put yourself into the position of the teacher. If someone is interested in what you are doing, your best bet is to share this book with them and let them get the information directly.

It is important to take time out for yourself each day to focus into your own spiritual awareness, drop away from the physical concerns of the day and, once again, become aware that you are spiritual, that you are divine, that you are—through the Soul—an extension of God. These quiet times with yourself are your time for communication between you and your God. They are important times in your movement of spiritual inner awareness and in your awakening into the higher Light.

2
Meditation: The Inner Realms of Consciousness

*God is in heaven, there are greater realms,
you don't have to die to experience them,
and you can know the divine reality while
you live on this earth.*

There are many levels within the human consciousness. Although they blend together and often function as a whole, they can function separately. Through meditation you can become aware of these levels of consciousness and become more familiar with them. It's a process of self-awareness, self-knowledge, and ultimately, self-realization.

It is difficult to know God until you know yourself. And you cannot know yourself until you take the time to find out about the levels of consciousness within you. The process of meditation is a useful tool in becoming aware of yourself. The following meditation takes you through the inner levels of consciousness and explains what you may perceive and experience on each level. After reading it through, you may want to take fifteen to thirty minutes to practice this meditation and experience for yourself the inner worlds—the last frontier.

As you sit quietly and close your eyes, start relaxing and moving into yourself. Some people feel as though they are tumbling over backwards. Some feel that the room around them gets smaller as they seem to move away from it. Others feel the room getting very big as they go deep within it. These sensations are all indicators that the consciousness within you is moving. Your own movement of spiritual inner awareness is taking place and you are conscious of it.

As you start moving back inside, one of the first areas you will encounter you is the sub-astral realm within. You are still very close to the physical world, and the imagery from when your eyes were open will be transferred to the inner eyelid. You'll see a reverse image or an outline of the last thing you looked at physically. You have to wait for this image to fade out, so that it does not distract you.

As you move further into your own consciousness, you'll find that the first level of the astral contains a blend of physical and astral images. You'll see some of the strangest looking designs, and that lets you know you're on your way. Light flashes may streak in front of your vision. Sometimes you'll see weird wallpaper-like designs and little squiggly patterns. These are all primarily the physical phenomena of the eye, the pressure and tension of the eye. It's often the fluid in the eye moving back and forth that causes those patterns. So don't think these patterns necessarily have any spiritual or psychic significance. These are usually indicators that you have a level of tension disturbing your vision. You don't have to kid yourself with these spiritual exercises. You can have the experience of these inner levels and there is no need to fool yourself and therefore block your awareness of the real thing. Be an observer and check out all the possible illusions.

One of the first indicators that you have tapped into the astral consciousness within you is that your imagination becomes very fertile. You'll start seeing all sorts of scenes and pictures and people. Now the challenge appears—to observe and not get caught up in the images. If an image appears and then disappears, rather than saying, "I wonder what that was?," trying to make it reappear in your consciousness, questioning why it appeared there in the first place, or wondering what its symbolism was, just observe it, let it go and keep on moving.

Continuing within, you may start seeing lights: circular lights, triangular lights, square lights, colored lights, etc. All this indicates that you are moving further within. People who have taken psychedelic drugs experience this level readily because the barriers that separate the physical and astral realms have been broken down; these people can flip into the astral realm very quickly. There's nothing wrong with that, but it's not a controlled action; it is not something you can do by choice. Spiritual exercises teach you to lift and expand your consciousness in a directed and self-controlled way. Rather than breaking down the natural barriers that are set up so that you can function in this world, spiritual exercises strengthen your ability to move into the inner levels with awareness and freedom.

As you go further in your meditation, the challenge remains to observe without trying to control your experience or get involved with what you are seeing. You're seeing the world within you. You may start to see some beautiful, fantastic shapes and designs. If you watch carefully, you can start to see whole scenes appear in the inner vision. It might appear that you're back in King Arthur's court at his round table. Just observe; it could be one of your past incarnations reflecting through the astral realm. Don't get distracted wondering if you were really there because that does no good. You must release that action and that image, regardless of what it is.

The question always arises, "Was that my imagination or was it real?" And the answer is always that it doesn't make any difference because you're not stopping there anyway. All you're doing is observing. What you see has value even if it's just your imagination. Even if it doesn't reflect a physical reality, it is still expanding your consciousness. It's stretching your mind out beyond its usual range. And this is the action we're after at this point—the reaching out with the mind and expanding the inner consciousness so that you can fill it with a greater Light awareness.

It's not unusual for people to meditate twenty or thirty years and never get further than the astral consciousness. They may develop a communication with their own inner guide, which could be part of a past incarnation process. They may think that they have reached an inner Master, but the Master forms do not work on the astral realm of Light. For the most part, what you experience in the astral realm is you working in those areas, you working through many of your own illusions, hallucinations, and fantasies.

The process is one of not being distracted or caught up in what you see. If you see a pretty flower, you don't have to pick it. You're really just a visitor to that realm—a very special visitor in a very special land—and you don't disturb or pollute the environment. You leave it as you find it so there is no trace of your presence other than contentment, peace, and harmony.

As you travel further into yourself, you'll come to the next realm, which is the causal realm. This level is denoted by the emotional quality present. The astral (imaginative) blends into the causal (emotional). There isn't a hard and fast division. They're intertwined. For example, if you are experiencing a horror movie inside of you through the astral consciousness, as you move more toward the causal realm, the emotions will come in to protect the consciousness and block out the horror. It may block it by fear or doubt or worry or distraction. Your job is cut out for you; you just let the horror movie play through your mind, your imagination, and your emotions until it says, "The end." Then you say, "If I have my choice whether or not to look at that movie again, I prefer not to." You let it go. Then you can move on rapidly.

The imagination is extremely powerful. It is where you've been creating and living in your daydreams for so many centuries and lifetimes that you're almost habitually restricted to this level. When you can't get beyond the astral realm, you feel as though you're not getting anywhere and you may doubt your inner meditation. Traversing your own inner realms of Light as taught in this exercise can be a very valuable technique to move beyond the astral level.

When you're involved in this meditation, you may get as far as the first part of the emotional level within you when some part of you just shocks you back to the physical world. Your eyes fly open and you're sitting there wide awake, breathing heavily, feeling a little confused and fearful and wondering what happened. You were rejected from what you were doing. The best thing to do at that point is to get up and do something physical—take a shower, do the laundry, do whatever is next on your agenda. It may not be beneficial to go back into meditation right then; that may compound the emotional confusion. Give it a chance to dissipate. Drink some water (an inner baptism). Break all these things loose. The next time you go in, the movement is faster because a lot of the same pictures and faces reappear. You look at them and say, "Yes, you're familiar," and keep moving further in.

You may reach the point where you can relate to the imaginative area readily and consciously, and because it is so familiar, you feel content. You could probably spend the rest of your meditation career there, without even reaching the emotional, mental or etheric levels. Many people say, "I have found Heaven within, and it's fantastic," and they have only reached the high astral realm. Once you learn what the imaginative level is, you can create within it and have those creations reflected back out into the physical environment. But you had better really know how to create, or you might create some emotional disturbance that comes back with the other creations.

When you go into the emotional or causal realm, you may experience some turmoil because earth is a planet of negativity. You must persist, so when the emotions appear, you affirm the Light action, saying, "This is fine. This is Light—just a different shade and quality and degree of Light."

As you go deep into the causal realm, you start moving into a very blissful feeling. This is where most people who meditate stop because they feel that *this is it.* It is such bliss to sit in your own body, aware of it in an unusual sense, but also feeling that you have transcended it so that you're not aware of any of its functions or needs. You're in a state of rapture.

Continuing on further, you can bring healing to your emotional body. By focusing on the various parts within you that seem to be disturbed and then sending this tremendous rapture of beingness through those emotional disturbances, you can bring balance to yourself. It is on this level that you can start to feel the balancing of past actions taking place. The release may be of an emotional quality. As things are stirred within your consciousness, you may find yourself crying or throwing up or something of this nature. This level can release tremendous things from the body. Don't let these experiences stop you. Handle whatever comes up and then go do something else. Come back later on and do the meditation again. When your consciousness is releasing something that is out of balance, the body may react as part of the release. Then it comes back into balance and you move on.

If you've ever gone on a fast or a diet, you'll recognize the pattern of imbalance followed by rebalance. For a few days the new diet or fast seems to work pretty well, but then the body starts reacting, and you think, "Am I really doing the right thing? I'm feeling *terrible*. If this was working, I would be feeling better." That's not necessarily so. Your body may be dropping away the imbalances caused by the foods it was addicted to, and it now must adjust to the new diet. People who go on fasts and diets are often attempting to tune the body up to be a better receptor of whatever they feel they want to receive. The same approach is one motivation for meditation. And a similar pattern happens. As purifications take place on the various realms, the consciousness does become a better receiver for Spirit. As you consciously take the Light into your inner world, the Light cleanses and refines each level. In the causal realm, your emotions become lighter, not only lighter in the Spiritual Light, but lighter in gaiety and joyfulness. The emotional qualities of past actions that caught you into desire patterns are dispersed. They just drop away. As the imbalances and turmoil are cleared out, you find that you can sit back and watch both your emotions and your imagination—the astral and the causal realms—interrelate in a sense of oneness.

Your challenge is to move on into the mental area. As you start entering the mental realm, the patterns of the mind start coming into play with thoughts like, "Why am I wasting my time doing this?" You'll think, "I wonder if all this is really true? I wonder if I'm really doing anything? I don't know if anybody else can do this; I don't know if I can do it either. I'm probably wasting my time. I should really go do something else more worthwhile. But...well, I don't know." That's the way the mental level starts. You go through this, saying, "All right, have your fun." You sit back and observe the mental action. Don't interfere. Don't stop it or say, "Be careful." Don't say anything. Just let it go. When this process has finished what it's going to do, just keep moving further and further beyond that verbal mental level.

As you go further, you'll find yourself deep within your own beingness; you will be moving into the intellect of your consciousness. I'm not talking about the brain or the mind. I'm talking about the *intellect.* As you move into this area, you will sense and experience "365 degree vision." I know a circle is 360 degrees; this is more. You'll see all around, above and below, a total spherical pattern. When you reach that place, don't ask questions. As soon as you do, you move yourself back into your mind or your brain. In the intellect, you don't have to ask anything; you just see what's there. It is all brought right

21

to you, and you simply observe. You don't have to go anywhere. You don't have to do anything. You don't have to search. People who reach the level of pure intellect often think that they have found the Supreme God because there is no question to which they cannot have the answer, and there is no knowledge that they cannot observe. People wonder what good it is to reach that place of pure intellect if you cannot ask any questions. You ask your questions *before* you go there. When you first sit down to meditate, you ask whatever you want, while you are still functioning through the mind. There is really only one question and that is, "Will I know my self-realized state now?" Then move into meditation.

These deep inner levels do not always transfer or translate into the physical world. As you start coming back out through the levels into the physical world, the intellect that was present so dynamically gets channelled down through your mind, your brain (your tape recorder), your emotions and your imagination, and it comes out in words that do not express its essence. The intellect itself is difficult to translate in English. The right words just don't seem to exist; you find yourself apologizing to people for your inability to put words on what you're trying to say. Sometimes you find yourself saying, "Look, I know I don't have the words, and I know when I say this, it's not going to really tell you what I experienced, but..." and you do the best you can because you have to start somewhere, endeavoring to let others see and know what is happening with you inwardly. Even if you fail to find the "right" words, you may convey the essence through your intention and the reality of your experience; your willingness to share may open another person's awareness so that they can move toward their own experience. If you didn't say anything and just sat back and said, "Well, you're too dumb to understand so I won't bother to explain," then you haven't even given them a chance. Not only that, you haven't given *yourself* a chance. Be willing to share with people. When someone asks you a question, you may find information you didn't even know you had coming through your mind and into your vocabulary. Maybe it's coming very purely from the intellect. As you practice traveling back into your inner levels, you gradually clear the way for more conscious access to those levels. While you are aware in your physical body, these experiences of tapping into your inner levels can happen.

There is one more level before you move into the Soul, and that is the etheric. You can recognize this level in a number of ways. You may suddenly feel as though you are falling through a great, empty space with no reference points, which for many people can be frightening. This level is a repository for many of the images, wishes, thoughts and dreams that you have created in the other levels of your consciousness but not acted on. Because they had nowhere to go, they are stored here, in the etheric. There is no sense of order to the way things are stored on this level, so part of the experience can be odd combinations of images, thoughts or feelings that make no sense together—yet they are familiar to you. You put them in there, but not in the way you may perceive them as you move through this level. The etheric can easily toss you right back into the physical if you react with fear or concern. If you continue observing, you will move through this seemingly confusing, strange area, through a level of nothingness that can seem terrifying to the cosmic mirror, the final barrier before you move into the Soul. This area reflects back to you the incompletions and attachments of the lower levels; if you get hooked into what you perceive, you spiral right back down to those areas. For example, you may come across the image of the boyfriend, house or car you always wanted (and haven't yet gotten). You start thinking about it and feeling those longings again, and there you are, back in the body with your feelings and thoughts. Always, observing rather than reacting, wondering, or getting involved with what you experience is the key to your freedom and ability to keep lifting and moving on.

These levels—the astral, causal, emotional, mental and unconscious—all exist within you. Yet they are only part of the whole; there is more. All of these levels also exist *outside* of you, including many levels within the Soul. Beyond the fantastic state of the intellect and the final test of the etheric, there is the Soul. In Soul, you are the It of Itself. You are eternal. You are Light everlasting. You become and are and recognize that you are the Alpha and the Omega, the Sarmad, the God of creation. In that realization, you know that you are these things on the realms *within* yourself. Many people who have this experience think they are the Supreme God, not realizing that they were only within their own consciousness. When you are in your inner universe, you are working through patterns by yourself. You may imagine someone else as a symbol to help complete a past action, but you are primarily working with yourself, by yourself. In your own inner travel, you can sometimes release conditioning from the unconscious and blocks that you have placed in your consciousness as you live your daily life.

You can go back into these realms by yourself whenever you want. You can do this by using a mantra or through a form of initiation. But if you are going to traverse the high realms of Light—the *outer* realms of Light—and go into the Ocean of Love and Mercy, which is reflected in the inner consciousness, you have to know the keys to move away from the body and into those outer realms.

In MSIA, The Movement of Spiritual Inner Awareness, you can become an initiate of the Traveler. Initiation is a somewhat foreign concept in the western world, yet it is an ancient spiritual tradition. Initiation with the Traveler is a choice to complete your experiences in this physical world, know your own Soul, and return home to God. When a person comes to this time in their existence, their prayer is heard, and they will usually find their path crossing that of a spiritual teacher, master or guide who can take them on their next steps. Every Soul has a unique path. Those who are ready to move back into the Soul are usually on the path of Soul Transcendence. The Traveler is a spiritual force that knows this path and is a guide to those who are ready.

In MSIA, initiates into the Sound Current with whom the Mystical Traveler is working are shown how to release themselves into the Soul body *first*, rather than traveling through all the lower levels to get there. You learn to move directly into the Soul realm of the outer worlds, and then to come back and pick up the sheaths of the outer realms that are of such tremendous dimension, yet undefinable. When you do this, you may find yourself traveling with lots of people. And that is one way to know whether you are traveling in your own inner realms or on the outer realms. When you're in the outer realms, the Mystical Traveler is with you, and other people are also present. When you're on your own inner realms, you are by yourself for the most part. Either way, there is nothing to fear.

It's important to realize that when you are in the Soul body within yourself, you are in a self-realized state. You have self-realization. But there are degrees of self-realization. Residing in the Soul body of the outer realms gives you a much higher, grander vista than residing in the Soul body of your own inner realms. This outer Soul realm is the abode where you truly live; it is your home. You are already on the Soul realm, but you may not be aware of it. In your own inner realms, you can be on the Soul, etheric, mental, causal, or astral realms. Through inner meditation you can experience the consciousness of those realms. But to experience these levels of consciousness on the *outer* realms, you must travel into those areas and become familiar with them. It's similar to traveling through this physical world and becoming familiar with it or traveling through your own inner worlds and becoming familiar with them. It's a matter of practice.

The work of the Mystical Traveler is usually not within your inner worlds. The Traveler's work with you is in the outer worlds, the invisible worlds of Spirit, to show you the way into a oneness with God. To reach that oneness with the Lord, you must go beyond the unknown of the unconscious where you may simply feel lost. You must go beyond the mind that says, "Oh, it's all a bunch of baloney and it's just not for me." You must go beyond the emotions that say, "That hurts too much; I can't stand that." You must go beyond the imagination that throws images up in front of you that can distract and delay you. If you stay with those things and they work for you, that's fine. When you come to the point where they're *not* working for you anymore, then—and this is a plea as well as a challenge—sit down with yourself and, maybe for the first time in all your existence, find out what is going on with you. Get down to the basics. Ask, "What is it that I need?" Then work in your need level. It can be hard; some part of you may say, "But I want and desire...." Those wants and desires are where you produce your biggest problems.

As you let go of your wants and desires, you start coming closer to God. You will eventually drop the desire to know God, reaching a point where you have no desires even on that level. Up to that point, you need desires to push you toward the inner awareness of Light. The desire level becomes a tool, an instrument that you control and direct. You create your own illusions to assist you in going up, and when that illusion no longer works, you let it go and create another one.

You are God, the creator, the Divine on all the levels of your beingness. There is responsibility that goes along with that. If God has infinite expression, and It does, then you are an expression of God. It is your quality of utilizing this creativity that sets you apart in your spirituality and in your ability to move your consciousness where you want it, when you want it, and to do with it as you wish. As you move your consciousness toward God, you create a happy, full life for yourself on this physical level, using your time wisely, assisting others, and being of service. At the same time you are securing yourself in the Soul realm and moving back to the Supreme Godhead, the Source of all.

3

The Breathing Meditation

In the meditation of "The Inner Realms," I described the levels within your consciousness and what you might see or experience as you travel there. That technique is primarily a passive meditation. Now I'd like to share with you a more active exercise that can be used by itself or in conjunction with the meditation of the inner realms.

The focal or anchor point of your attention in this exercise is your breath. By focusing on your breath, you maintain an awareness of this physical level while you move into a state of deep relaxation and traverse the inner realms. The action of the inner realms can be confusing, and with no reference points, you can get caught up there. Watching your own breath provides a reference point for you. If you have been passive in your meditation, you must become active again when you come back to this physical world. That transition can sometimes be difficult. By adding an active element to the passive meditation, you remain active throughout and do not have to make that adjustment when you come back to the physical level. The Soul realm is active, also, so it is difficult to reach it from a passive state. The active exercise of breath awareness makes it easier to reach into Soul.

You can do this breathing meditation anywhere, at almost any time. It is particularly good if you are in situations where you are experiencing stress or anxiety. The breathing meditation calms you and brings in self control and direction that is most beneficial. It quiets the body, the emotions, and the mind, but does not put you to sleep. Instead, it brings you to a greater state of alertness and awareness. It shifts you to a brain wave frequency that allows greater control over your immediate environment, if that's what you feel you need. When you are through doing this spiritual exercise, you will have moved into a quiet state, and you can carry this quiet with you wherever you go. No matter what situation you're in physically, you can be in a state of calm and quiet inside yourself. This peaceful quiet often becomes infectious to other people around you; they'll look at you and sense your calmness. The peace you carry within you can quiet others as well, more than you can imagine.

This technique is very useful when there is turmoil around you, if someone has yelled at you or attempted to diminish you in some way, or if you've been in a traumatic, testing situation and aren't happy with the way you handled it. The best course of action is to bring yourself into an inner calm so that you become master of yourself.

I suggest that you do this exercise for fifteen to thirty minutes at first until you master it. Then you can do it as long as you need to balance the situation that you wish to balance.

Technique

In this breathing meditation, sit comfortably with your eyes closed, ask to be surrounded, protected, and filled with the Light for the highest good, and focus on your breathing, in and out. This is your reference point; this is your focal point. You may find your breathing slowing down tremendously. You may even wonder when you took your last breath. When I do this exercise, I often find that I breathe only once every four or five minutes. In a relaxed, calm state, your body has no need for large volumes of oxygen. But your body will still be breathing within the higher consciousness.

You can focus on your breath at the stomach chakra, the chest, the nose, the throat, the mouth— wherever you sense your own breathing. You might not focus on any part of your body; you might just sit and be aware of your breath. You don't need to have any thoughts at all. For the greatest benefit, breathe in through your nose and out through your mouth. If you have to cough or clear your throat, go right ahead. This does not disturb the meditation. Many times it is a way to release pressure from your body.

If you come to a block in the flow of energy that doesn't seem to release, continue concentrating on your breathing. Keep track of that as your reference point. You may start to hear sounds within your consciousness. Don't let that distract or bother you. Keep your attention on your breathing. You may start moving within your own consciousness, and then find yourself completely back in the physical world. It's easy to feel that you're not getting anywhere when this happens; don't let that stop you. This exercise allows for an inner and outer motion. Go right back to your breath again. Focus on your breathing. You may find that in the first five minutes or so, you move back inside yourself pretty well; then within the next ten minutes or so, you fidget around and try to find out where you were. Maybe you lost track that you were doing a breathing technique, and instead you were trying to pick the daisies along the way or look at the beautiful lights. These are all illusions and distractions to the process. This exercise is one of quieting yourself. As you become more quiet, these things will cease being a distraction.

Twenty minutes of this meditation can make you feel as though you've had a good night's sleep. If you get up in the morning and still feel tired, you might take five or ten minutes to sit and refocus yourself on your breathing. This can assist you in getting the energies within your body circulating in an aligned way so that you can have a productive, active day.

If you start having dreams or focusing on images while you're doing this exercise, you have lost track of focusing on your breath. You can experience some strange things during this meditation as accumulated tensions and conditioned blocks break away.

The release can cause unusual images to flash through your consciousness. There is no need to react. Just keep focusing on your breathing. You may feel your head getting lighter and lighter, as though you're being lifted up. This is your consciousness expanding. You may start rocking back and forth with the energy of the Light that is present. Don't try to stop it. Your job is very simple: focus on your breathing. If the energy keeps that rocking motion going, it's okay. You may also feel activity in the third eye area of the forehead between the eyes. Don't get caught up in that sensation. The best technique is to keep focused on that which is most familiar to you—your own breathing. You are using the familiarity of your breath as your reference point while you travel into your own inner realms.

The idea is that whatever you see, whatever you hear, whatever sensations you feel, whatever you experience, you hold your breathing steady and use it as your point of concentration, your reference point that remains constant as all other things shift. You'll be surprised at the peace and calm that can result from this exercise.

4
The Sacred Tones

In the Bible, it is written that God spoke the Word and there was Light; the Bible also tells us that the Word was made flesh. That first Word that brought about creation is the name of God. When the Word of God is spoken, it sends out energy currents that bring about changes in the structure of electrons. It changes creation. The spiritual essence condenses and materializes. This word or sound is a very powerful force; it can also be a very subtle force.

A mantra is a specific sound or tone which, when spoken or chanted, can invoke a spiritual essence. A mantra can be said out loud or inwardly. People often see me sitting very quietly. I may look like I'm sleeping or resting but I'm not. I'm chanting the name of God, raising the frequency of my body. This is different from lifting outside of the body and being in the spiritual oneness, which is relatively easy. To actually raise the frequency of the physical body, you have to bring an element of upliftment into yourself. As you repeat the pure sacred tones within yourself, you become that word, that frequency. When you have become that, you have lifted yourself into another dimension.

Many groups use mantras as a form of meditation. Mantras, or tones, are sounds that originate from various dimensions and planes of being. Some originate from what we call the lower worlds—the astral, causal, mental, or etheric realms. When chanted, these tones lift you to the level from which they came. Most of the tones I teach originate in the pure realms of Light—the Soul realm or above. When chanted, they invoke the essence of perfect purity—that which is blameless, sinless, pure in all ways.

As you chant sacred tones, you bring the essence of purity into yourself, and that purity begins to replace the negativity that is often within. These tones are tremendously powerful. Changes will occur in your consciousness as you intone them. If you are serious about making Spirit a working reality in your life, I suggest that you chant fifteen to thirty minutes a day. Regular practice can bring about noticeable change.

As you chant these tones, several things may occur. Every person has different experiences. I'll explain some of the things that people have experienced so you'll feel more familiar with them should they happen to you. You may experience things that are similar but not precisely the same as what I describe. You may have entirely different experiences. It's important to keep in mind that if you don't experience what I describe, the tones may still be working for you. Every person is unique and individual. So it follows that everyone's experience with spiritual exercises is also unique. The spiritual exercise reflects your reality. Your experience is your own, totally valid for you. Don't try to make the experiences I describe happen for you. Just use them as a reference point.

It may seem as if nothing is happening for you in these meditations. It's important to know that, so you don't place expectations on yourself and then feel a sense of failure or disappointment. These tones are from the invisible realms of Spirit and are working for you spiritually. It may be that you are simply not able to recognize what is happening on the higher levels yet; it doesn't mean there is nothing going on. As you practice these meditations, you are attuning yourself to the higher realms, and building a bridge of awareness between these high places and the physical world. With practice, you will become more familiar with your own inner realms and the outer realms of Spirit, and begin to bring that awareness back into this world if that is for your highest good. The important part of all this is your intention to check these meditations out by doing them to the best of your ability and tracking your experience. Then observe. Give yourself enough time to work with them. Be patient. Be devoted to your own upliftment and unfoldment.

Three Master forms work with these tones. They may appear in either of two ways: you may *hear* the tone, the sound of God, independent of your own chanting; or you may *see* the Light form of the Master force that is working with you. You may see the form as a point of green, blue, or gold Light. If you see purple, you may be seeing the energy of the Mystical Traveler Consciousness, which is formless and goes beyond the Master forms that work with the tones. The Light may appear to be about twelve to fifteen inches in front of your eyes. You may see a face within the Light, although this is rare. As you move your awareness out toward the Light, you can exteriorize your consciousness. If that happens, you may hear a pop or snap as you step free of your body. Don't let that startle you and don't be afraid. Just go along with it. You may feel yourself lifting up in consciousness. If you feel a tingling or pulsating sensation in your third eye area or the crown chakra at the top of your head, this can mean that you are exteriorizing from those levels of your body. You might feel pressure in your head or eyes. Your vision may seem a little blurred, and you might even feel a little light-headed. These are all possibilities and I'm describing them to you so you are not distracted by these experiences.

When you are done with the exercise, you can chant the "E" a couple of times as described in Chapter 1. You can also drink some water, and cross your feet or legs to ground yourself and bring yourself back into alignment, ready to function in this physical world.

Because these tones originate from the highest realms of Light, they tend to draw your consciousness up. It's important that you do not use these tones while you are driving a car or working around machinery. They should not be done in any situation where you need your full conscious attention and focus.

HU

The "HU" reflects an ancient name of the Supreme God. It invokes the purity of that perfect God. It may be chanted in several ways. One way is to separate it into its letters "H" and "U," chanting a long "H..." and then shifting to "U..." If you are chanting out loud, take in a deep breath and, as you breathe out, chant "H..." "U..." If you are chanting silently, you might intone the "H..." as you breathe in, and the "U..." as you breathe out. Another way to do this is to pronounce the "HU" as one syllable (pronounced "hugh") and chant it as you breathe out.

After you call in the Light for the highest good, a very effective way to work with this is to do some deep breathing before you begin the chant. Breathe in and out five times, feeling your body fill up with the Light energy on each breath, bringing yourself into calm, into your center, as you breathe. After five breaths, begin the chant by breathing in and chanting the "HU" as you exhale. Do this for five breaths. Then repeat the process: five breaths without the chant and five with the chant. Repeat it one more time, so that you chant the "HU" fifteen times in all. This will build up terrific energy. Once you have done the series of fifteen, I suggest waiting at least fifteen minutes before you do it again. You probably won't want to do this more than twice each day.

This tone can be chanted silently, as an ongoing chant, at almost any time and place *except* when you are doing something that requires your complete attention, like driving or operating machinery. It can be very helpful in centering yourself and bringing yourself into balance.

Remember to ground yourself by doing the "E" (see Chapter 1), drinking some water, and stretching a little when you are done.

ANI-HU

The "ANI-HU" is a variation of the "HU." If you are chanting out loud, you would intone "Ani-Hu" as you breathe out. If you are chanting silently, you might chant the "ANI" as you breathe in and the "HU" as you breathe out. You can also chant the entire tone as you breathe out. You may find yourself doing it one way today and the other way tomorrow. These tones are given to you with flexibility in how you work with them. Work with them in the way that works best for you.

The "ANI-HU" chant is also an invocation to the pure one, the Supreme God, but it has an added dimension that brings in the quality of empathy with others. As you chant this tone, you will find that quality of empathy increases. For this reason, it is a beautiful chant to do in a group situation, as a continuous, rolling sound. In a large group, it can begin to sound like "And I - You" or "You - and I" … "ANI-HU".[2]

HOO

The "HOO" (pronounced WHO) is a very similar frequency to the "HU", though slightly lower in vibration than either the "HU" or the "Ani-Hu."

---

2. For more information on the quality of empathy that is brought in with the "ANI-HU" chant, refer to MSIA Soul Awareness Tape #3004, "The Law of Empathy".

Some people will feel more of an attunement with one, some with the other. They may be used interchangeably. The "HOO" is chanted as one syllable; in a group, it would be chanted as a continuous, rolling tone. While you are chanting, place your focus and concentration in the center of your head. This will lift the scattered energies of your body (sexual, physical, emotional, and mental) and bring them into greater balance.

If you are feeling scattered and wanting a greater sense of oneness and alignment inside, this tone can be helpful. If you can take a few minutes by yourself to call in the Light and silently chant the "Hoo," you may find the scattered feelings dissipating and being replaced with a sense of inner peace. For the best results, it is helpful to hold your focus in the center of your head.

You can do these tones for very short periods of time at first, gradually building up to longer sessions, just as you would with physical exercise. You might start with 2 or 3 minutes, and build up to 10 minutes, 15 minutes, and longer. I suggest that you eventually do spiritual exercises for 2 hours each day. Many people feel that is impossible; they could never fit 2 more hours into their already busy schedule. Spiritual exercises tend to restore your energy rather than deplete it. Because of the energizing benefits of these exercises, you may find yourself needing less sleep. Some people get up a little earlier in the morning, do their spiritual exercises, and find themselves more rested and energized for their day than if they had slept. This is an individual process. Be patient and consistent with yourself as you find what works for you.

Doing spiritual exercises is an alive process, and what works for you may change over time. Perhaps you build up to doing an hour of s.e.'s daily, and find that working so well for you that you stay with it for awhile. Then you start noticing that you don't feel complete after an hour, or you very naturally stay in meditation a little longer than an hour. Pay attention to both the quality and quantity of how you do your spiritual exercises. My suggestion is that you relax and do them with devotion and loving, and with the intention of receiving the value that is for your highest good.

Remember to ground yourself by doing the "E" (see Chapter 1), drinking some water, and stretching a little when you are done.

5
RA Meditation

The RA tone is as old as the first word that was ever uttered. It carries a lot of energy. When you are first learning to chant this tone, the power it invokes into your consciousness can make you feel a little dizzy or nauseated. I suggest that you don't do it too many times. This is a good tone to use if your energy is low and you need to get it flowing again. It's good to use when you're doing something that requires extra physical strength or energy, like moving furniture or lifting something heavy. It can really bring strength and energy to you in a hurry.

This tone is best chanted out loud while you are standing up. It's good to do it in front of a mirror if you can, although that isn't necessary for the success of the exercise. The word is "RA, pronounced like the cheer, "Rah, rah, rah!" To be effective, it has to be intoned in a particular way. Take a few breaths to quiet and center yourself. Ask for the Light to be with you for protection and guidance and to bring forward the highest good. Take a deep breath, hold it for a couple of seconds, and then, as you exhale, chant out loud, "ERRRRRRRRAAAAAAA." As you finish, completely exhale any air that's left in your lungs. Exhale everything, until you feel like you're almost going to cave in. Then take another deep breath and repeat "ERRRRRRRAAAAAAA." And exhale completely again. Repeat this pattern once more. After the third time, breathe normally for a few seconds. Then repeat the whole process, chanting a set of three RAs. Do this for three sets of three "RAs." Three sets of three is the most I suggest you do at any one time because of the power of these energies.

When you do the chant, do it loudly and forcefully. Feel the air rushing out as you chant. Feel the power of that word. Chanting this tone with vigor will enhance the power you feel in return.

You may sense the power and the energy that has built up with the chanting in a number of ways. You may feel your fingers and hands tingling with the new energy you have brought forward. You may find unusual things happening to your vision as the energy comes in. You may see flashes of color or light. Your vision may fade and then return. If you put your hand up about six to twelve inches from your head, you may be able to feel your aura, the energy force field that surrounds your body.

As a variation, you might want to try standing with your arms relaxed down at your sides. As you inhale, raise your arms up to the side, keeping them straight, until they come together above your head. Then as you exhale and chant the "ERRRRRRRAAAAAAA," keep your arms straight and move them back down to rest at your sides. You will feel the power and energy increase even more doing it this way, and you may feel the force field around your body expanding to fill the whole space that your arms describe.

This exercise can expand your aura, increase your circulation, and bring vitality and strength into your physical body and your consciousness. This is a powerful chant, yet the energies can be subtle. Since you are dealing with spiritual energy, which is invisible, you may or may not be aware of the results of this exercise in the physical. You may simply notice that your energy level has improved and held steady for longer than usual. Be an observer and find out how it works for you. This may be obvious, but the powerful energy you invoke with this tone is to be used. You would not do this exercise and then sit or lay down to relax, read, or do something of a quiet nature.

Remember to ground yourself by doing the "E" (see Chapter 1), drinking some water, and stretching a little when you are done.

6

So-Hawng
Meditation

There are frequencies that you can chant that unify the mental and emotional vibratory rates. These help to solidify you where you are, so you can lift into yet a higher consciousness. To prepare to do this chant, come into a quiet position for meditation and ask that the Light work with you and allow only that which is for the highest good to take place.

This tone is done mentally, silently. One part of the tone is a mental frequency and the other part is an emotional frequency. You say the first part of it when you are breathing in and the second part while you are breathing out. The tone is "SO-HAWNG." You breathe in, inwardly chanting "SO," and out, silently chanting "HAWNG." You'll find that the chant starts fitting itself in with the rhythm of your breathing. You may experience unusual feelings in your physical body; you may even feel like you're getting asthma. If the emotions have been shackled, the tone starts shaking them loose. Keep on going.

These things that have been blocking you will eventually be released, and there can be an exhilarating feeling that comes over you from the freedom you are gaining inside of you, and from the frequency of this tone.

The "SO-HAWNG" takes the mental thought patterns and the emotional patterns and brings them closer together. Have you ever had a feeling without a thought to match? Maybe you just feel like crying and can't think of any reason to feel that way. Or you feel depressed but aren't able to pinpoint why. This can be miserable because you can't seem to do anything to change it; you can't even identify its source. The "SO-HAWNG" meditation is helpful in this kind of situation.

The reverse situation happens, also, where you have a thought, but no matching emotion. You know that you "should" work on that special project or do that tax report or clean out the garage, but you have no matching feeling to give you the energy or enthusiasm to do it. A thought without a matching feeling—a feeling without a matching thought.

The "SO-HAWNG" balances the mental and emotional energies with each other and brings them into harmony, making it easier for you to be productive and active in your daily life.

Chant this tone mentally, at your own rate. You might want to chant between five and ten minutes or however long you intuitively feel is right. If you feel a disturbance come in, let it go and keep chanting in rhythm with your breathing. If you need to cough or clear your throat, go ahead and do that. It does not disturb the meditation. Be natural; that's part of the action of this meditation.

When you have finished chanting, quiet your mind and drop into a few moments of silent meditation, observing what comes into your consciousness and releasing it all into the Light for the highest good.

Because of the balancing nature of this meditation, you may feel terrific when you are done, ready to get up and handle your day. If you need to, however, do the "E" as explained in Chapter 1. You can also drink some water and stretch a little to ground yourself.

7
THO Meditation

The word "THO" is a very powerful word that can be used as a mantra to bring healing to the body. It has been used since ancient times by mystery school masters to bring in a healing vibration. When you intone the word in the correct way, you pull to yourself a healing vibratory rate. It increases the energy that is with you and brings a flowing power into your consciousness. This word is a sacred word, as are all the tones and exercises taught in this book. They are not to be taken lightly or used for purposes other than the upliftment of your consciousness.

As with the other meditations, you begin this one by coming into a state of quiet, asking the Light to surround, protect, and fill you and that the meditation bring to you that which is for the highest good.

To bring forward the healing frequency, the tone must be said a certain way. It's almost the same idea as a voice graph. If the right person—one who knows the "key"—says the right word, they can open the vault. The same word said incorrectly will have no effect. The tone "THO" said incorrectly will have no effect. Said correctly, it is extremely powerful.

This tone is combined with a pattern of breath control. The tone and the breath control are equally important to the whole effect. You breathe in deeply and hold the breath; then exhale fully. You may find that this tone is most effective when you breathe in through your nose and out through your mouth. You breathe in again, hold it, and exhale fully. On the first two breaths, the exhalation should take about twice as long as the inhalation. The third time, you breathe in deeply, then exhale forcefully, sharply, saying out loud, "THoooo." The emphasis is on the "TH" sound, with the "oooo" sound trailing. "TH" is a sharp, percussive sound. The "oooo" sound is held for a few seconds, and then you exhale completely, emptying your lungs as best you can. Breathe normally for a minute or so and then repeat the whole pattern: three deep breaths, holding the air in for a few seconds and then exhaling fully, saying the tone "THoooo" on the third exhalation. Breathe normally for a minute and then repeat once more.

I suggest that you repeat this tone no more than three times in any one session. If you're doing it correctly, you will feel a tremendous power build up in just three repetitions. It is best to do this exercise out loud to learn it and attune yourself to it. Once you sense a strong attunement with this tone out loud, then move into doing it silently and continue building your attunement in that way. It carries great power when done silently as well as out loud.

When you have finished the tone, close your eyes, rest quietly, and observe the inward action. Since this is a mantra of healing, you may very well see the color green. Green is the primary color that comes forward. You may also see some gold or blue with the green. In some cases the green blends with the blue and the color looks turquoise. It will often come in swirling patterns, creating different shapes and whirls of energy.

This tone brings in a healing power which, at first, is condensed primarily around your head. You may feel this as pressure, pulsating, dizziness, light-headedness, and so forth. As you sit quietly and let the power work, it will come down through your body and concentrate on those areas that are in need of healing. It works through all levels of your consciousness to bring it all into balance. If you wish, you can direct it into those areas that you feel are out of balance by focusing your attention onto these areas and seeing them healthy and perfect. Don't direct this energy to your eyes, however. It is already concentrated in that area, and an extra "dose" can make your eyes go out of focus and make you feel dizzy.

As you sit in quiet meditation after intoning "THO," you can picture other people in your creative imagination, and this healing power will go to them, also. This mantra is a powerful force. It alters the energy patterns around your body. If you find yourself in tense situations at work, for example, you might want to do this tone inwardly. It may very well start altering the energies around you, and things may become more calm and more balanced.

Remember to ground yourself by doing the "E" (see Chapter 1), drinking some water, and stretching a little when you are done.

⊹⊹⊹

Remember that you never, ever use these sacred tones of God to force a control pattern on anyone else. Use these tones for your own balance and your own upliftment, and always use them under the protection of the Light and the highest good. If that brings balance and upliftment to others around you, that's great. If you use these tones with the intention of controlling anyone else, then you have entered into black magic. That action will come back to you to complete, and you might not like it. You are held responsible for your actions. Do yourself a favor and don't enter into that area. Work with these tones under the protection of the Light to bring yourself into greater health and balance, to expand and lift your consciousness and to assist you on your path of upward evolution toward God realization.

8
Ranging

Ranging is a technique that is used to scan an area and perceive what is there. When you do this technique, your consciousness acts like a radar screen. Ranging is a psychic exercise. You don't have to be spiritually attuned to work it. This is a beautiful exercise, teaching you that you are multidimensional and that you have tremendous potential within your consciousness. In this exercise, you extend your mental energy out and perceive through it. Ranging is an age-old method, and it's very effective. Some ancient civilizations used it as an effective early warning system. It can be used in similar ways today.

It's probably best to start out simply and learn this technique in easy steps. Remember to start this exercise, as with any of them, by asking that the Light surround, protect, and fill you, and that only that which is for your highest good take place. Then you can relax, knowing that you are protected and safe, and you can flow with your experience.

A good place to start is by learning to scan the room you are in. Close your eyes and project your consciousness up to a point above your head. You can do this by imagining that you are lifting up above your head and looking around from there. At first you may think that this is happening only in your imagination. With practice, you will become aware that your consciousness is truly moving into the areas that you "imagine."

Some people see themselves lifting above their heads, so that their point of view of the room is a foot or so above their normal physical point of view. Other people feel themselves lifting up, and sense the room from this new perspective. There is no "right" way to do it. Have fun exploring how this works for you.

Once you have lifted your consciousness to a point above your head, send out a beam of Light to one corner of the room. Again, it may seem like you are just imagining this at first, and that's OK. Then rotate the beam to the next corner, and then the next until you have touched to each corner of the room. What are you picking up? You may see or sense images. You may feel sensations in your body, like cool, hot, rough, smooth, bumpy, etc. There's nothing to do with the information; for now, just note what you perceive.

When I'm lying down watching TV and I want to know what time it is, but I'm too lazy to turn my head and look at the clock, I'll shoot my consciousness up above my head, rotate it, and scan the clock. It won't be as clear as when I am looking at it physically, but I'll get the impression or image of the time. If I want to verify the information, I'll turn and look at the clock physically—and if it's within a minute or two, I consider that a success.

You might want to scan your house to see who is in which room and what they're doing. Then go check it out physically to see if you were accurate. For awhile it might be more of an imaginative process than a reality process; but as you keep doing this, you will find that you can screen out the imaginative elements and learn to recognize what is real. Your accuracy can become astonishing.

The basic idea of the ranging technique is to project your consciousness up to a point a foot or two above your head. Then you send out a beam of Light from that point and begin to rotate that Light beam around. When you're first learning this, you may rotate it slowly. As you become more skilled, you'll rotate the Light beam faster. Eventually, you'll rotate it so fast that it will look like a solid circle above your head. People who are clairvoyant see this as a golden circle of Light above your head. Like the spokes of a wheel turning slowly, you can see the individual Light beam when it rotates slowly. But when a wheel rotates rapidly, you see the spokes as a solid image, just as the Light beam appears solid when it rotates rapidly.

When this Light beam that you are rotating encounters something—a disturbance, an event, a shift in energy, you follow that beam out to the source of the disturbance and perceive what it is. When you follow the beam out, do so for just a split second; less than that, really. You pick up an image or an impression without breaking the cycling process of the beam. To stop and perceive would be a distraction. You check the impression while the motion of the radar screen continues. Then as you return to that spot, you check it again. You are actually building a series of still images which you are seeing in such a rapid sequence that they they blend together as a "moving" picture.

You have to be very aware of yourself and how you are feeling to be accurate with this technique. If you are scanning your home and start feeling sick to your stomach, you need to know whether or not that feeling is yours. Before you start scanning, check your own levels to find out if you are feeling clear physically, emotionally, and mentally. If you're not feeling clear on some level, take a moment to iden- tify the areas of your disturbance so you have a baseline to work from. Then, if you pick something up during the exercise, you'll know what is yours and what is someone else's. If you're clear and you start feeling sick during the process of ranging, you might want to go check with your family and see if anyone is feeling ill.

Sometimes when you're ranging and picking up information, you're perceiving things psychically. Events may appear psychically before they appear physically. Keep a written record of your impres- sions. If you pick up a stomachache, but everyone in the house feels fine, write that impression down along with the date and time. That stomachache may appear physically in a few hours or a few days. Keeping track in this way can assist you in verifying how this technique works for you.

When you are successful in scanning your room or your home, you may want to expand the area of your ranging to include the grounds of your house and maybe a few blocks surrounding your home. Through this technique, you may start to pick up on friends who are coming to visit before they get there, or on your spouse coming home from work, or on the kids playing outside the house.

Many parents are intuitively tuned in to their children. A parent may be in the house, but if their child gets hurt three blocks away, they know it. Or if their child gets into a fight, they know something's wrong. They're ranging unconsciously. We can all do this process to some extent unconsciously. This technique expands that innate ability so you can do it with awareness.

As you gradually expand the dimensions of your ranging, it becomes more and more important to keep a record of your impressions and the images you perceive. The more territory you cover, the more complex it all becomes. You may start ranging on a statewide or nationwide basis; if so, using maps to give you a visual image of the areas involved can be helpful. As you extend the ranging to the city, the state, the nation, and the world, you start tuning in to all sorts of things. When you're out long distance ranging, it can be very hard to differentiate between a state and a nation or between one country and another. So check the newspapers carefully for awhile to see what's happening and how it's matching up with your impressions. Start compiling a log. As you record your impressions, you may at first seem like a "raving idiot," but with practice, you will be able to start screening out reality from illusion.

Maybe one day in your ranging you sense an earthquake somewhere in the south. You might write in your log, "Earthquake—possibly Mexico or South America." Then you read in the paper two days later that an earthquake took place in Chile. You check your log and find you were correct in your ranging experience. If you lived in Oregon and the earthquake took place in California, that's still an accurate perception. With practice you'll be able to pinpoint locations more and more precisely. At first, locations may be pretty general.

One thing to watch is taking something from within yourself and projecting it out onto something else. For example, psychics have predicted great earthquakes for a particular time period and then personally experienced some trauma or illness during that time period.

A few years ago there was a psychic who predicted a tremendous earthquake for California and created a fear pattern among those who took her seriously. Right at the time she had predicted the earthquake, she had a heart attack. That was her earthquake. In a sense, she perceived the event accurately, but she took her perception of a personal experience and projected it as an outer event. In that sense, she was inaccurate. So learn to differentiate between your inner experiences and those that are taking place in the physical world. How do you do this? Tracking your perceptions in a journal is a key. You will develop a sense of what you are perceiving by writing your impressions down and checking them with physical events.

Be the "super-scientist" with all this. Observe as clearly as you can. Record your observations. Keep looking. Check the news. See where it matches your ranging. If you miss, that's okay. Be honest and admit you missed, but keep track, because you might find out later on that you were really on target. There is very little that you can't tap into psychically. Many years ago I was ranging and saw a book that had been written by a South American professor—a book that would make a great contribution to the world. I told some people about it, and they tried to find the book, but were unsuccessful. Because of that, they questioned my credibility. I found out later that the book had indeed been written, but had been suppressed by the government and copies were not available.

You can kid yourself with your impressions. You can get caught up in illusion. You can tap into your imagination and mock up all sorts of images. But if you're honest with yourself, you'll be the first to know when you're in illusion because you won't be able to verify the findings. As you keep a log and read the newspapers and check out immediate impressions with family or friends, you'll know if you're dealing in reality or imagination. It's important to realize that there is a reason why you imagine what you imagine rather than imagining something else. Maybe you are tapping into a higher psychic realm where something is in a completed state, but has not yet precipitated physically. It may not take place for another nine or ten months. This is why you keep records. One day you may be reading the news and recognize something in a news item. You go back in your journal and find a record of that occurrence written months earlier. Time is a relative thing. These events and your perception of them may take place simultaneously on the realm where you perceived them, but they may take place in different timing in this physical world.

With practice, you can become extremely accurate with your ranging. Maybe the first two thousand times you won't be successful, but eventually you can be. If you want success, keep at it. When I first started doing this, I forgot what I'd seen on the scan probably the first hundred times I did it. But then I started remembering. When you really tap into something, you may get a feeling of exhilaration inside, and maybe a little feeling of fear. Just pull your beam back and bypass that fearful area. When you feel balanced, extend it out again. Go at your own pace. Don't feel that you have to become an expert today. This can take years of practice.

Keep in mind that, as with every technique, you use this for the highest good. That means that you do not use this to violate the privacy or the consciousness of any other person. If you use it to become the local "Peeping Tom," you'll find the action coming back to you in strange ways. You do not get off free. If you misuse this technique, you accrue karma to yourself, and you will be held accountable for it. Use this technique for your own upliftment and progression, and for the upliftment of others. Then you'll be in good territory.

When you work with the ranging technique, scan with your eyes closed. There will be less distraction from physical objects and movement. I suggest that you do this for no more than fifteen to twenty minutes a day. The sensation of quickly rotating the radar screen can make you feel dizzy, or you may get a headache. The increase in energy can cause these sensations. Stop the exercise and bring yourself back to regular physical consciousness, grounding yourself with the "E" (see Chapter 1), drinking some water, or stretching a little.

While you're ranging, you may actually feel your consciousness turning within you. Your astral body may try to turn with the scan, and that can cause some very peculiar feelings. It's sort of like riding a roller coaster. You might see or feel all sorts of things. Keep on going—stopping is a distraction. When you do stop, finish the exercise, and go on with your regular physical routine. You may or may not want to work with this technique on a regular basis. The abilities that it develops can be useful, and the proof it can give you of your potential for multidimensional awareness can be very valuable.

9
Flame Meditation

You will need: a candle taller than it's holder
a clock or timer

The flame meditation deals with the very specific, powerful energies of fire. Fire is always a two-edged sword. It can be used for great good, as when it is used to provide warmth, to cook food, to decorate and to beautify. You may have experienced the comfort of sitting by a warm fire, and how relaxing it can be to gaze into the flames as they flicker and burn. This comfortable quality is one part of fire's beneficial side. But, out of control, fire is one of the most destructive forces that exists. So I approach any meditation that uses fire as its focal point with extreme caution and suggest that you always use respect for the force with which you are working and common sense in your handling of the fire.

You will need a candle that is tall enough so that you can clearly see the flame above the candle holder. Other than that, it really doesn't matter what type of candle you use: tapers, columns or little votives. They're all fine. The candle should not be set so deeply in a holder that you have to look down on the flame. You should be able to clearly see the flame while you are looking forward.

For the meditation, you can either hold the candle so the flame is at eye level, or set the candle on something that puts the flame at about eye level. It's better to find a place to set the candle down, eliminating the risk of dropping the candle as you move into the meditation. Never do the flame meditation in bed or where there is a high fire danger. Always blow the candle out as soon as you have finished the part of the meditation that uses the flame.

You may also want to put a clock where you can easily see the time that has passed, or set a timer. Once you have a candle and a place for your meditation, light the candle, sit down and get comfortable, and invoke a prayer of Light for your own protection, asking that the meditation bring forward those things that are for the highest good. You may want to play some soft music in the background. Although it's not necessary, this can help you hold a point of focus and be a reference point for the rhythm of your mind.

Begin gazing at the candle flame, placing your consciousness forward into that point of light. Observe what takes place in and around the flame, and observe the sensations and reactions in your body. It is very important that, while you are gazing at the flame, you do not allow yourself to slip into a trance-like state. It's easy to do with this exercise. You need to keep the energy flowing forward and out toward the flame, or keep it flowing up. Don't allow your energy to drop down within your consciousness. If you feel your energy starting to drop or fade back inward, blow out the candle and stop the meditation immediately. These energies are not to be misused. The trance state is not the most positive or uplifting state of being. It will not bring about the positive release of emotional karma, for which this meditation is designed. It could, indeed, compound the karma and confuse your consciousness. So it is extremely important that you monitor this potential carefully and keep your energy flowing up and out—and that you stop the meditation immediately if you feel your energy dropping inward. You'll know. You'll be able to feel it if you are slipping into a trance. If you can pull the energy back up and focus it outward into the flame, that's fine. If you can't, stop the meditation.

The flame meditation is designed to release many of the emotional areas of your consciousness. It's a good meditation to do if you have been feeling irritated, upset, angry or otherwise out of balance emotionally. While gazing at the flame, these emotional areas may begin stirring within you, and you may enter into powerful feelings of disturbance and despair as the turmoil of your life is brought up to be purified in the fire of Spirit, which the flame symbolizes. You may experience many, many feelings. Just observe them, hold your concentration on the flame, and release any feelings into the Light. Become a neutral channel through which the emotions can flow out and be cleansed. You may feel a pulling or pulsating sensation in the area of your eyes, between the eyes, and in your head. Your eyes may tear. Your vision may become blurry. It's all part of this process of releasing and lifting into higher perception and awareness.

As you gaze at the flame, it may shoot up very high or flicker almost violently for a time, and then burn back down again. There are a few possible causes. One is that there is something in the candle wick that is causing the flickering. You may want to change candles if it distracts you. If it's not the wick, it may be that you're blowing on the candle as you breathe out, causing the flame to flicker. Put the candle far enough away from you so you don't blow on it, and breathe gently so that there is no disturbance. If it's neither the wick nor your breath, it may be the energy present that is causing the candle to flicker and burn with an unusually tall flame. It may just be the power of your consciousness as it is projected into the flame. As you project energy into the flame, you may be able to make it shoot up several inches and then bring it right back down again as you redirect your energy. This can give you an indicator for what you are doing.

The candle flame burns off extra amounts of energy. This is one reason why it's nice to have a candle burning in your home. It burns and transmutes excess energy. It's particularly helpful when people are expressing emotional turmoil of some sort. When this is happening, they are releasing excess energy into the environment. Having a candle burning can help to balance them and keep you from picking up their negative energy.

The flame has an energy field, and as you gaze at it, you may begin perceiving the colors of this field. You may see the colors on the outside of the flame, closely following the shape of the flame. Or you may see it as a circular glow encompassing, but also extending beyond, the flame itself. You may see it as a circular glow at the tip of the flame or in the heat pattern above the flame. The primary colors you'll see are green, blue, and red; as you tune into the spiritual frequency, you'll also see purple. You might even see a rainbow of colors within the flame.

There is a devic force that works with the flame. It is a life force, a consciousness that is from the devic kingdom (which is a lower part of the angel kingdom), and it is part of the fire's existence. Remember the Bible story of the prophet who was thrown into the furnace to burn? An angel appeared and protected him so that he was not harmed, even in the midst of the fire. This was a form of fire elemental or fire angel. They exist, and they have dominion over fire. They can control it and all its functions. There are people who are attuned to these fire forms and who can work with them. I've known people who could take burns away from the body because they worked with the fire lords. The people of ancient cultures almost always worshipped fire gods. In Hawaii, the god of the volcano, a form of fire god, was worshipped. These forces do exist, and communication with them can be established.

As you gaze at the candle flame, you may see the fire deva appear as a little figure, almost human in shape, but made of fire. It may appear to have arms, legs, and a head, flickering and twisting as the flame does. It may appear to be transparent. You may see it along the edge of the flame or at the tip, even sometimes slightly above the tip of the flame or in the darker area of the center. It may appear and hold steady for a moment or it may just flash in momentarily. Some people have described the "little man" as having a head and arms, but no legs. Some have described him as an unusual light within the flame that flickers from one side to the other. Others have seen him in such detail that they've even seen the features of his face. Everyone's experience with this is a little different. You may see him or you may not. If you do, these descriptions are a reference point for you.

The only restrictions people have are doubt and lack of confidence in their own ability to do all things. There are no restrictions on your consciousness, which is why you can move into these meditations and have success. The consciousness of the fire deva is restricted. It must stay within the energy pattern from which it takes its existence. But you can move your consciousness there and tap to its beingness. You can communicate with it on its terms. You can move into any energy pattern and perceive it directly. You are god; not the Supreme God, but a direct extension of God. You are flexible. You are multidimensional. But you must develop your awareness of the totality of your beingness. These meditations are valuable because they expand your awareness of all the levels of your existence and increase your flexibility in traveling from one state of consciousness to another.

Practicing the flame meditation can directly affect your dream state. It will usually heighten your awareness of your dreams, and you may bring back much greater memory of your dreams than you normally do. Your dreams may be of an unusual nature after doing a flame meditation. You may dream of fires, and you may feel emotional turmoil within your dreaming. Don't be disturbed. The emotions are releasing. You are receiving emotional balancing. That's one of the greatest values of this technique.

Because this is such a powerful technique, I suggest that you approach it cautiously. The first time, I suggest you do it for no more than five or ten minutes. The energies this exercise brings in and the karmic patterns it releases are much more dynamic than you may be used to handling. Do the meditation for five or ten minutes, then watch your dream pattern and your emotional balance closely. If things are a little unusual or shaky, don't do the meditation again for several days. Give things a chance to settle back down. Then do it again. If everything seems to be flowing along okay, go ahead and do the meditation for a little longer. Then watch your dream patterns, and if things are shaky this time, wait for a few days before doing the meditation again. As you become accustomed to these higher energies, you'll be able to hold the meditation for longer periods of time, and do it more often. I suggest that you never do the flame meditation for longer than twenty minutes a day.

As you watch the flame, you may find yourself moving into an almost dreamlike state. It's okay to follow along with the images that come forward, as long as you keep your energy flowing up and out. Observe the images, and direct them outward toward the flame. You may be reminiscing about your life, moving backward through time to when you were a child. As you keep going back through memories of when you were younger and younger, you may suddenly run out of this life and into another one and find yourself remembering things that did not happen to you in this lifetime. You may be tapping into the Akashic records, which are the records of all your existence. If you get caught up in memory patterns, just flow along with them. As the images and memory of your past existences appear, let them go. Release them into the flame and see your consciousness purified and cleansed.

When five or ten minutes are over, or you feel your eyelids dropping, or your consciousness moving back inside of you instead of out toward the flame, blow out the candle, sit back and drop into a quiet meditation. With your eyes closed, observe whatever appears on the screen of your inner eye. Keep your legs and arms uncrossed so that the energy can flow freely. You may see odd shapes or forms or strange lights. Just let it all float through. You don't even have to wonder what they are. You may see the flame deva during this part of the meditation. Acknowledge its presence and send it Light and love. If you see images of past lives during this part of the meditation, bless them and yourself with the Light and let them go. This process can bring about great healing and balance.

After a few minutes, you will intuitively feel the energy of the meditation lifting; the meditation is over. Remember to ground yourself if you feel spaced out and find it difficult to move around. Review how to use the "E" tone in Chapter 1 and do it, drink some water, and stretch a little to realign your energies and get you anchored back down on this physical realm. Or you might want to chant a few "RAs" to energize you. Experiment and find what works best for you.

10
Water Meditation

You will need: two 4 or 5 oz. clear glasses
water
soft lighting

The physical body has an electromagnetic force field around it, and if you tune into it, you can detect the energy. Some people see the energy; others feel it. A number of research groups have been studying and photographing the energy patterns of the body. Using special films and techniques, they have taken pictures of the energy as it comes off the fingers or other parts of the body. They have recorded a difference between the energy patterns of people who are sick and those who are healthy people, emotionally balanced or upset people, and frightened or calm people. Different physical, emotional, and mental states of being affect this field of energy. There are many variables that change and alter the electromagnetic force fields of the body. The results of this research have removed any doubt about the existence of this electromagnetic energy. With practice, you can become more aware of it, and learn to tune into it and the colors that it emanates.

In the water meditation, we use water as a focal point for discerning this energy. In this exercise, it is easier if you have a point of focus outside yourself with which to relate. As you place your consciousness and your attention into the water, you begin to build the power of the magnetic force field, and then you are able to perceive it more directly. You may sense the electromagnetic energy or feel it or see the auric colors or the etheric body. By building energy around and in the water, you magnetize the water. You actually change it with your energy. You may be able to detect this change through the altered taste of the water. When the water has been magnetized, it is in balance with your energies and drinking it can be beneficial to you.

To do the water meditation, you will need a 4 or 5 ounce clear, untinted glass. It can be any shape as long as you can hold it comfortably. Fill the glass half or three-quarters full with your regular water. Find a place where you can sit comfortably for fifteen or twenty minutes. Part of what will be happening during this exercise will be you shifting your vision so that you can see the other vibratory frequencies. You can't see them with your normal vision. If you could, you would already be seeing auras, the etheric body, and so forth. But you can see these when you alter your vision somewhat. Bright lighting may tend to keep the physical environment too sharply in focus, so you may find it helpful to turn the light low or sit with your back to any source of light so you will not be distracted by it. If you wear glasses, try doing this exercise with your glasses on and then again with them off. Some people prefer one way; some the other. Whatever works for you is fine and does not affect the purpose of this exercise.

Before you start this meditation, take a small sip of the water to taste it. Try to remember what it tastes like so you'll have a comparison later when you finish the meditation. You might want to keep another glass of water aside as a reference point. It would be best to have it in another room as your "magnetic" frequencies might affect it also.

For the meditation itself, hold the glass of water in both hands. Place your eight fingers around the front of the glass, away from your body, with your fingertips close together but not touching. Place your thumbs around the back of the glass, toward your body, so they are close, but not touching. It's important that you don't overlap your fingers as this will short out the magnetic energy.

There are two lines of magnetic force or energy that travel through the body, one on either side. As soon as you cross your hands, you short-circuit them, just like crossing electrical wires shorts them out. If you keep these lines open, however, the energy will continually flow and will be able to increase in power. For the same reason, you will want to have your legs and feet uncrossed.

Hold the water glass at about the level of your navel. You can hold it out away from your body or close to it, whichever is more comfortable for you. As you hold the glass, look down and gaze into the water. Focus your eyes on the water, but expand your awareness to include the rim of the glass, the spaces between the glass and your hands, your hands and your arms. Relax and keep intensity out of your gaze. Just hold your concentration steady.

Be aware of anything in your physical surroundings that might affect what you see in the glass or in the water. Notice any sources of light or colors in your clothing or environment that might be reflected in the glass or water. Check out all aspects of your physical environment so that you're not fooled into thinking you're seeing something psychically/spiritually when you're not.

Once you've taken care of those levels, begin placing your focus into the water. Become aware of the energy in your hands as they surround the glass. Be aware of the energy that is transmitted between your hands. You may start to feel a tingling sensation in your hands. Your eyes may begin to water or burn as you project energy out from them. You may feel a tingling or a pulsating sensation around or between your eyes. This is all natural with this method. You're working with energy in a way that you may not be accustomed to, and that may be more powerful than usual.

I suggest doing this exercise for ten or fifteen minutes at first, to give yourself enough time to build up the electromagnetic energy and move beyond the levels of physical vision and perception. That may seem like a long time. Don't be concerned if you've "had it" after five minutes or so. Remember that you are working with very strong energies in an unusual way. If fifteen minutes is too long for the first time, let it go and come back to it later. With practice, you can gradually build up to doing the exercise longer.

You might see a number of things as you gaze at the water. The first thing you might see is a bluish-purple haze around your hands. It might look like wisps of smoke. That may be part of your etheric body. The etheric body is a body that is parallel, in a sense, to your physical body, but existing in a higher vibratory rate and a more refined state of being.

You might see a white light, like a cloud or a mist, coming around your hands or around the glass. Then, beyond that, you may begin to see colors— the colors of your aura. The colors that usually appear first are green, blue, and red, but not necessarily in that order. You may see one or more of these colors. When you're tuning into the spiritual force, you may begin to see some purple. You might see the color in the water. Sometimes it will appear to flicker on the surface. Sometimes you'll see it deep in the water. Or it might appear on the edge of the glass, or between the glass and your hands, or around the hands. Or the hands themselves may appear to turn a different color. There are many possibilities. When you look directly at the glass, you may see the color on the side of your hand. As soon as you look directly at it, it seems to disappear because you focused your physical vision on it. Don't focus; just gaze. Don't set up any expectations. Observe what appears. As you continue to gaze at the water, your physical vision will shift and you will begin to perceive traces of color appearing.

The visual image of the glass and your hands may shift from "positive" to "negative," and look like a film negative. That's part of what's taking place.

Continue to observe. Don't try to control it. Allow whatever is taking place to happen; your job is simply to observe.

As your consciousness shifts within you, you may find your visual perception of the glass changing. Your consciousness may exteriorize from the body, and, as that happens, you'll "see" the glass and your hands becoming smaller and smaller. That's okay. You may find your perception of color is heightened at the same time. Or if your consciousness moves toward the glass, you may experience a sensation of "falling" into the water. You may see a face or image in the glass, looking back at you. These things mean that your consciousness is moving. It's not being restricted by the boundaries of your physical body. You're learning and practicing expanding your consciousness. You're learning and practicing freedom.

As the physical vision shifts to psychic vision, there may be moments when the image at which you're looking disappears entirely. Your eyes are open, but you're not seeing anything. That's okay, too. Don't be concerned. Hold steady. It'll take care of itself. The hands and the glass may go in and out of focus as the magnetic energies fluctuate. It's all part of the experience. It's all valid.

When you have done this exercise for five or ten minutes, pause and take a sip of the water. See if you can perceive a difference in the taste since you began the meditation. Then continue the meditation, and be sure to taste the water again when you have finished. You may experience subtle changes in the taste of the water. Sometimes, particularly if the water originally had a bitter or chemical taste, the change will be obvious. You might not see anything and still have tremendous success with this technique because part of it is taking the magnetic force of your own body, increasing it, vitalizing it, and placing it into the glass of water—actually magnetizing something outside of yourself with your own magnetic energy.

Listen to you as you work with this water meditation. Let your intuition guide you. Don't be too rigid in your approach. If your eyes are burning uncomfortably, close them for a few minutes, and then resume gazing at the water. If you feel tension building in your neck or shoulders, close your eyes and rest your neck and head. Then continue on.

If you want results, do persist in doing this technique. Some people try this exercise for three or four minutes; nothing happens so they say, "I didn't see anything." And they give up. That's all right if you want to give up. Some people are more naturally attuned and they get results very quickly. Those people are the exception rather than the rule. The rest have to sit and watch, maybe doing this meditation many times. With practice, they gradually develop their ability to tune in. In other words, you have to be stubborn enough to follow through and not let your own irritation or discouragement control you. As soon as your eyes start watering or burning, as soon as your vision starts shifting or altering, it's very easy and very human to give up. That's fine, if that's what you want. It's all up to you to work with this in the way that allows you to experience what is available in this meditation.

Don't get your ego involved in working with the water. As soon as you do, as soon as you grab for an experience, you stop it. You may sit there and gaze at the water for five or ten minutes. If you think, "How ridiculous," you may never experience any-thing—except feeling ridiculous. But if you sit there and think, "Okay, I'll go along with this. Let's see what happens," you have made yourself available and can have an experience with it. It's another technique to draw you into your inner self.

When you have finished the meditation, take a few minutes to close your eyes and sit quietly. Watch what appears on the "screen" of your inner eye. Don't look when you do this. Just see if anything shows up.

The water meditation is a technique that can change your consciousness, if for no other reason than you don't know what to expect and can't predict what's going to take place. This frees you from the demands and expectations of your mind. You get beyond the mind and your consciousness can start flowing and working for you. If you feel your analyti-cal mind start coming into play, you might want to slowly take a deep breath and let everything go as you exhale. Relax—but don't drop the glass. If it helps, give your mind an anchor point. You might want to play some soft music for the mind to focus on, to help you relax and be quiet mentally.

Remember that, when you are working with this type of meditation, if you say you can't do it or that it won't work, then you have created that possibility for yourself. That's your restriction. Your only re-striction is what you create. If you say it can't be done, then it can't—for you. But this meditation has been done by many, many people, and their success is proof that it does work. You don't have to do this meditation with any great belief factor. You don't have to tell yourself that it will work. You don't have to tell yourself that it *won't* work. If you just do it in a neutral consciousness, as a scientific observer, to see what might take place, you will have your own experience within it.

11
Introduction to Color

In ultimate reality there is only Spirit, Sound and Light.
These are the ultimates.

The Bible tells us that in the beginning there was the Word. That was the Sound. And God said, "Let there be Light," and there was Light. The Light was created by the Sound. The two forces are as one, and they are one with Spirit and one with God. These are the primary forces that dominate all aspects of creation. All things have been created by Sound and Light.

There is a level of positive Light energy that we call the Holy Spirit. It is the life force that sustains everything. Here on earth, the Holy Spirit cannot be seen, heard, felt, or perceived in any way. It is pure. It is invisible. It is the highest manifestation of God's beingness that extends to earth. It is the Spirit that pervades all levels and realms of Light, all forms of life, all beingness.

In the higher realms, there is only this pure energy of Spirit. There is no other manifestation of

Light except the Sound, the audible Light stream that extends into the heart of God. In the realms of Light below Soul (etheric/unconscious, mental, causal/emotional, astral/imaginative, and physical), the Light becomes denser, less pure, more affected by other elements. When the Light comes into these denser levels, it is split into different energy frequencies or rays, which become color. The pure Light coming into this environment is bent and altered so that it becomes color and is able to be perceived by the physical senses. The primary colors as we know them are aspects of the pure Light energy, altered so that they can be perceived on this level.

All Light on the physical realm is perceived for the most part as color. The colors are actually an illusion. Spirit is the reality. But since the personality cannot perceive Spirit directly on this level, it sees Spirit as energy rays of color. Each of the color frequencies is under the direction of a keeper of that Light ray. These beings are intelligent, highly sophisticated spiritual forms whose job it is to bring each color into a physical frequency and to make the power of that color available to humanity. These masters function in the negative realms of Light, but that does not mean they are "bad." As mentioned earlier, the positive realms of Light are the realms of Soul and above; the negative realms are the levels below Soul. If you think of this in terms of the two polarities on a battery, it may make more sense. Both the positive and negative poles are needed for the battery to function. The negative pole is not "bad." It is part of the whole, with its own characteristics.

In this physical world, it is best to learn to use all aspects of your environment for your upliftment. While you may not perceive Spirit and Light directly from this level, you can learn to perceive the colors in their purest form. You can learn to contact the masters of the color rays, and you can learn to use the power of the color rays for your upliftment.

This part of the book is designed to give you some knowledge of the color rays and the masters that direct them, to teach you how these color rays can be used, to suggest techniques for attuning to the colors, and to develop your ability to work with them.

12

Attunement to Color

There are colors everywhere in our environment. Some are obvious and easy to perceive. It's easy to look at a friend and see what color shirt or socks they are wearing. It's easy to see the green leaves of a tree, the rich brown of the earth and the bright colors of balloons at a child's party. In your home you may paint the walls of your bedroom pale green, because that is a soothing, relaxing color for you. You may decide to paint the kitchen yellow because it's a bright, happy, uplifting color. There are other colors all around us, though they are more subtle and difficult to detect. Some people never do see these more subtle colors, while others see them occasionally, and some people see them often.

Have you ever looked at someone and seen a flash of green around their hands as they move? Have you ever seen a subtle glow of gold around someone's head? Have you ever awakened at night, opened your eyes, and had the room look blue for just an instant? What are these colors and where are they coming from? These subtle color energies signify specific things and are with you when you are involved in certain areas of expression, though you may or may not be aware of them. We'll talk more about this later.

If you want to become more aware of these subtle colors, their presence, and their significance, there are some general techniques that can heighten your awareness of the colors themselves. Each technique is designed to help shift your vision so that you see more deeply than usual. As you practice these techniques, you may begin to see colors that you don't ordinarily see. Practicing some or all of these techniques is a great way to attune yourself to the essence of the subtler color energies. You can practice these techniques frequently; the more you do them, the greater your awareness will be of the world of color around you all the time, though you may not be aware of it.

As you practice the techniques in this book to heighten your color awareness, be aware throughout your normal, everyday activities of any evidence of color that you have not experienced before. You may not have experiences immediately; the results can happen at any time. You may feel that you're not having much success with the techniques, and then "suddenly" see a beautiful, glowing, radiant blue around your partner as the two of you are watching television. The heightened color awareness is not going to confine itself to just those moments when you are working with a technique. In fact, if you try too hard, you can block your awareness in that moment. Then, when you least expect it and you're not trying at all, colors may flash forward in your vision. So be alert, relaxed, and open to color awareness all the time.

After you practice each technique, I suggest that you record your experience in your journal. You may want to create a special section for your work with color attunement, devoting a section to each individual color as well as the different attunement techniques. Writing down your experiences can increase your awareness of what is happening around you and can help you to tune into color frequencies in an even greater way. It is a way of telling yourself, "Pay attention to this area. This is valuable to me."

Colored Paper Exercise

You will need: colored construction paper
                   one sheet each of red, orange, yellow, green, blue, purple, and white

For the best results with this exercise, you may have to experiment with the lighting in the room; vary it until you get the results you are looking for.

As always, start by calling in the Light for the highest good. Take your sheets of colored paper—red, orange, yellow, green, blue, purple, and white—and stack them, top to bottom, in that order, so that the red sheet is on the top and the white is on the bottom. Hold them so all you can see is the red sheet on top. Then take the red sheet with one hand and, holding the rest of the stack with the other hand, pull it slowly across the orange sheet, which is the next sheet down. When you have slowly pulled the red sheet all the way across the orange, set it aside, take the orange sheet, and begin pulling it slowly across the yellow sheet (the next one down). And so on until you reach the bottom of the stack. You can repeat this process several times the same way, or reverse the order so you start with the white sheet and move down to the red one. Or you can mix up the colors so that you do not always keep them in the same order.

As you are pulling each sheet across the next, focus your gaze on the place where the two colors come together. At first you may not perceive any shift in vision and, therefore, the appearance of no new shades or colors. But as you continue working with this technique, you may begin to see evidence of colors more subtle than the colors of the sheets themselves. At first you might see, along the line where the two colors meet, a heightened, brighter, more vivid shade of the same color. Or you may begin to see a third color where the two primary colors come together. You may experience an entire sheet of paper shift color and "become" another color. This means that your vision is beginning to attune to the more subtle colors that are all around, although not ordinarily seen.

As you work with these colors, your eyes may begin to burn or tear. That's a normal physiological reaction. If it gets too intense, just close your eyes for a few minutes and give them a chance to rest. Don't look around the room or at other objects because that will return you to your everyday physical vision.

You would then have to start over in your attempt to shift your vision into the deeper levels.

It's best not to set up any expectations for this technique. Just let whatever happens, happen. There are no rights or wrongs. There's nothing you're *supposed* to see. You're just practicing shifting your vision and perceiving color on a more subtle level. Whatever your experience, that is what you will be accomplishing.

Aura Attunement Exercise

You will need: a mirror
a black or white background
a black or white shirt
optional: a blue light bulb.

The human aura is a force field of electromagnetic energy that surrounds the human body. The aura, by its very nature, consists of color and movement. Colors reflected in the aura may be strong, primary colors, or they may consist of infinite variations and shades of color. There is a whole science concerning the colors of the aura and what they mean, and it is not our purpose to explore that here. However, you can attune to color by learning to sense and then see the colors of your own aura.

One technique for developing the ability to see auric colors is to sit in front of a mirror in your room or someplace where you won't be disturbed. Wear a neutral colored shirt, like black or white. It will help to put a black or white screen behind you. White poster board set against the back of a chair will do; a white sheet draped over something behind you will also work. If possible, dim the lights; better yet, get a blue light bulb and put it in the socket instead of a white bulb. The softer the light physically, the more chance you have of perceiving the light on other levels. If you can focus a blue light behind your head, that is ideal. What you are doing is attempting to remove as much physical color as possible from your immediate environment so that you will not be distracted by any color or light from the physical level.

When you're ready, sit and gaze into the mirror at your face and head. Let your gaze move around the periphery of your head, across the top of your head, down around your ears, neck and shoulders. You might want to focus briefly at the third eye (center of the forehead) area. As you start to feel energy in any particular area, focus your attention there briefly, then keep your gaze moving. When you focus intently on one area, you are likely to bring your physical vision into play and block the subtler vision. You may begin to see any number of colors for just a flash of time or longer. You may begin to see little flashes or dots of color that appear to be somewhere between your physical body and your mirrored image. If you begin to feel a heightened energy in your hands, you might want to glance down and see if there is color flashing around them. The hands are very sensitive and there is often evidence of color around them.

Water Meditation

The water meditation is a way of attuning your-self to the color frequencies of the electromagnetic force field around the body. By practicing the water meditation, you may begin to perceive the subtle colors of this energy. The meditation is very simple, yet powerful. See Chapter 10 for complete instructions.

✢✢✢

These techniques are for increasing your ability to perceive color. You can expand them or adapt them to your own needs. Keep in mind there is no right and wrong. There is nothing you are supposed to see. Nothing is good or bad. It is all just the experiencing of color and energy.

13
Color Rays of
Light

In the next sections, I will go over some information about the color rays of Light and the masters
that work with them. There are techniques to practice for each color ray to increase your attunement.
This is where you may want to use your journal to
record your experiences.

When you work with specific colors, there are
several approaches that you can take. Check them
out and use whatever works for you. You can also
adapt and mix the techniques. You might want to
visualize a particular color surrounding and suffus-
ing your body. You may want to visualize yourself
surrounded by a colored robe or cape. You might feel
a particular color wash over you like a wave. Maybe
you'll use a breathing technique and feel yourself
breathing in the color with each breath, drawing
that color into every cell of your body. You might
find a technique of your own that isn't mentioned
here. You can have a lot of fun discovering what
works for you.

Before you do any of these techniques, always
ask for the Light of the Holy Spirit and the Mystical

Traveler to be with you for the highest good, so that all you receive is right and proper for you. If you are working with a particular color, you can open your consciousness to the master of that color ray in a short prayer: "I ask the master of the yellow (or red or blue or whatever) color ray to beam this color through my consciousness to assist me for the highest good." Then sit back in a receptive position. All you have to do is accept. Nothing else is required. You don't have to believe or disbelieve. You don't have to see anything. You don't have to feel anything or know anything. Just be open to the experience.

Red

The color red is a vibrant energy, full of power and force. Red is a vitalizer for the body. It brings strength and a driving energy. For example, if you were physically not a particularly strong person and had to change a tire on a car, it might be very difficult or impossible for you to jack up the car with your own strength. You might find that, as you pushed down the jack, it pushed right back up against you so that you and the car were equal in strength. Or you might even find that the car was winning. By asking, "If it be for my highest good, I ask the master of the red ray to release its power to me," that vibrant energy associated with the red color ray could come in and vitalize you. You might then be able to successfully jack the car up and change the tire. The red ray is valuable in any situation where physical strength is needed, but the energy of that ray should be used very quickly because it is so powerful. You would only ask for it to be present when you need a sudden surge of energy. You wouldn't ask for the color red and then sit down in a chair to read a book. The power of the frequency could produce an imbalance in your system if not used immediately and forcefully.

To use the red ray effectively, you do something with it right away. You ask for it while you're in the process of using it because usually—through telepathic communication—you are already receiving the flow of energy before you get the request for it formed verbally in your mind. The master form of this red ray has often been present to assist when people are caught in life or death situations. You've probably read stories of the mother who lifted a car off her son when he was trapped underneath, or someone who rushed into a burning building to save children trapped there. There are all sorts of miraculous happenings that are the result of the force of the red color ray being used for extra strength and power.

The masters of the color rays are great masters, but because they are also in a state of evolvement, they may release a little more or a little less energy than you anticipated. So while asking for this energy, also ask for your highest good. This request will automatically filter the flow of energy so that you walk in a more perfect protection.

The color red has often been associated with anger or heavy emotions. It's true that when people are angry they have tremendous, explosive energy within them, even if they are suppressing the anger physically. And it is true that if you are feeling anger, your aura may be reflecting the color red. One way to work with this anger is to visualize a cooler color coming into your aura and body to neutralize the explosive energy you feel within. Asking for the blue ray for the highest good can cool your anger. This is just one example of the many ways you can work with the colors for your upliftment and growth. Knowledge of these areas and how to work with them can be tremendously valuable to you.

Meditations

1. At some moment when you are going to expend a great amount of physical energy in a short amount of time, ask for the master of the red ray to be present with you for the highest good. Visualize the space around you permeated with the color red. Breathe it in and feel it travel into all parts of your body, from your toes and fingertips up through your body to the top of your head. Then quickly move into physical activity and pay attention to any differences from how you normally feel.

2. If you are going to be involved in heavy physical labor, do the RA meditation, visualizing and breathing in the color red as you chant. This meditation is explained in Chapter 5.

Orange

The color orange creates a continuing flow of energy. Like red, it is also a color of high physical vitality, but of a more sustaining nature. If you were going to run several miles, you would ask for orange rather than red. In a continuing kind of activity the red energy would be too dynamic. You would want the strength of the orange ray so that you would continue flowing and flowing while that energy continued to come into you.

Orange would be used when you feel a little weary, a little tired. Maybe you're having the "three o'clock drops" and are feeling so tired you don't see how you'll ever make it to five o'clock. At such a time, you'd ask the master of the orange ray to release, for your highest good, the orange color into you.

Orange is connected with the energy of the sun, and some of the Eastern philosophies use this color to strengthen and vitalize the body. For instance, you can take colored cellophane and put it around a bottle of water. Set the bottle out in the sun for four or five hours, which allows the sun's rays to come through and vitalize the water, and then drink it as a tonic to the body. The vitalized water will go very rapidly into the nucleus, the very center of each cell, and start generating that color ray from the inside. Some of you have not yet experienced traveling through your own inner realms into the nucleus of each cell in your body. When you do, you'll find out that there is color there. Some of the colors can very readily be equated with the colors you see out here in the physical world, and some of them are colors you have not yet seen here.

Meditations

1. Ask that the master of the orange ray be present and release the power of orange to you, for your highest good. Consciously experience a heightened vibration of energy surrounding you. Visualize that energy as orange. As you take in a deep breath, visualize the color orange coming in through your nostrils, into your lungs and then out through your blood stream to every area of your body. Feel the color orange flowing out to all your extremities as well as filling up your chest area. Then continue with your normal activity.

2. Visualize a brilliant orange robe wrapped all around your shoulders and flowing down, across, and around your entire body. Feel the power of that robe reaching into you and infusing you with the power of the color orange.

3. For a few days in a row, observe your energy patterns. Take note of when your ups and downs occur, and how you're feeling generally. Then vital-ize a bottle of water with orange cellophane (as explained previously) and drink the water several times each day for five days. Observe your results and note any differences.

Yellow

The yellow frequency comes in as a mental process. It tends to qualify the intellect, although not entirely. The master of the yellow ray deals with the quality of understanding or thinking. Some people have equated yellow in the aura with being a coward, but often the one who is considered a coward has the ability to think a situation through, see clearly what is happening, and clear it verbally, rather than fighting their way out with their fists. The fighter deals with red. The "coward" deals with yellow. The longer the fight can be held off, the greater the "coward's" victory. The fighter can actually lose their rational consciousness from too much intense energy; the coward can keep the yellow color coming in to clear the situation through understanding. Often the so-called coward perseveres to the end and becomes the hero of the day.

The yellow color ray can be brought in if you feel like you are mentally out of balance. Ask for the yellow Light to come in for the highest good and bring the quality of balance to your mind. Yellow can also be used when you are reading a text in preparation for an exam, or it can be used while you are taking the exam to bring clarity in for your ideas and expression. You would ask the master of the yellow ray to release, for your highest good, the yellow ray to you.

If you were reading a book that was extremely complex or symbolic and found that you were not understanding it too well, you would ask the master of the yellow ray to bring that color frequency into you.

The yellow ray works as a clarifier; it tends to help you to lift your consciousness so that information becomes clearer and you can proceed with it. It's not a physical lifting, it is a lifting of your consciousness above the clouds of confusion.

The yellow ray diffuses rapidly; it just continually moves away. It's like thinking of something and wanting to tell someone about it, and having the thought disappear just as you are about to speak. That's how fast the yellow color ray can diffuse from your consciousness. So you may want to ask for the yellow frequency to come in and hold over your head area like a helmet. A person who is clairvoyant could see this yellow come over your head as you are residing in that ray. The yellow comes in through the top of the head, the prefrontal lobes, the thinking area of the brain. This brings a greater quality of understanding that may go more deeply than the mind can go; it may actually go into emotional understanding and it can help to clear and release blocks through this combination of emotional and intellectual understanding.

Meditations

1. In a situation where you need mental clarity, ask for the master of the yellow color ray to be with you for the highest good, and to release the color frequency to you for greater understanding. Breathe the color in through the top of your head and feel it fill the head area, infusing the entire brain with its color. Ask that you may use the color yellow to

perceive the situation in the clearest way possible, always for the highest good of all.

2. Visualize a helmet of yellow coming down and encircling your head area. Feel the helmet hold there; sense it as almost a tangible thing. You might want to put your hands up, and hold them several inches out from your head, and sense your hands resting along the edge of the helmet. Feel the energy in the palms of your hands, and feel the energy between your hands and your head. Visualize that energy as the yellow helmet.

Green

The master of the green ray is the keeper of a brilliant emerald green color. Once in awhile you will see it as a pale green, but usually it will be a deeper, more vibrant emerald green. This color has two actions: it's partly a teaching action and partly a healing action. However, the whole idea of teaching is actually healing, so there is really no difference. In the spiritual sense, both are called balancing actions.

The green works as a balancer—an educator, an adjuster, or a balancer. If you were going to lecture to a group of people on a very advanced area of theoretical science, you would probably want to work under the green ray. You would ask the master of the green ray to assist you in this teaching action, to assist in unfolding the information to your students.

If you have an area of your body that you feel is out of balance, you might ask for this color to be directed there. If it's a physical pain, the green ray may alleviate it. If it's an emotional pain, it can clear it. If the pain is brought on by electromagnetic changes, it can stop it entirely, right on the spot. This can be one way for you to know what level the pain is residing in and what has instituted it.

There is also a quality of life with green; green is a good color to use as you work with people. If you happen to be involved in soothing the pain of someone you love, and this pain is in the shoulder area, you might pat that person on the shoulder or near that area, visualizing the color green flowing out of your hand and into the shoulder for the highest good. You don't have to tell the person what you're doing, but you can bring a comfort and a balance in this way. As always, ask for the highest good when you work with this color.

Meditations

1. Ask for the master of the green color frequency to be with you, to release to you the energy of the color green for the highest good. Visualize it all around you, bringing balance to all areas, physical and emotional. With each breath, envision the color green flowing into your body and extending to all areas of your body.

2. Visualize yourself in a mountain meadow with green grass and ferns all around you. Set up the scene in as much detail as possible, but primarily feel and see yourself surrounded and supported by the color green, the color of nature. Feel, sense, and see the green grass underneath you and the green trees above your head. Feel the soft, calm green come into your body and bring you into perfect balance, physically and emotionally. You might want to play some soft music in the background as you do this meditation. Some possibilities are Canon in D by Pachelbel, Golden Voyage, Ani-Hu, Wind from Heaven by Jeff Gauthier.[3]

3. If you have specific areas of your body that need to be balanced physically, work with the green color ray. Ask that the master of the green ray work with

3. Ani-Hu and Wind from Heaven are available through MSIA. For further information, refer to Books & Tapes at the end of this book.

you for the highest good and then, using the power of your consciousness, send that color ray to the area needing balancing. Visualize the area as completely as possible. Visualize it being healthy and whole and perfect. You might envision the color green almost as a laser beam of green Light, traveling directly into the area needing balance. Or you might envision the color as a soft bubble of green Light permeating the area needing balance. Let the imagery unfold to you in the moment, but hold the focus of the green Light over the area. You might want to do this for up to twenty or thirty minutes at a time, depending on what you are attempting to clear.

Blue

The color blue is part of a spiritualized intellect. If you see this blue in someone's aura, be aware that the person is expressing in the area of Spirit and intellect.

Too much blue in the aura can cause a person to go into depression, actually "get blue." When you say, "I feel so blue," often it is because you have over-weighted yourself with this blue frequency; you're not quite in Soul consciousness, nor are you wholly in the physical world. You're in-between and you may not be able to correctly identify your reference points. So getting the blues is one way of knowing where you are, by way of disturbance or pain.

The blue frequency can assist you in lifting above some of the physical desire patterns of the earth. I'll present this idea from a man's point of view; women can shift it over to their point of view and it will also work. If a man sees a beautiful woman walking across the street, starts wondering what it would be like to have sex with her, and then gets hung up in the lust or desire area, the red in his aura will come shooting forward as an instant power, the strength to do something, to act. It is this action that has caused the color red to be identified as a debased color. People see the color red in the aura and may say, "That's dirty; that's disgusting." It's not; red is strength, power to expend the physical energy to have sexual intercourse. If you have trouble in the areas of lust and desire, and you feel that power come into you at inappropriate times and places, you can ask for the master of the blue ray to infuse you with this color blue, which brings the consciousness into a more intellectual-spiritual nature. This negates the whole lust pattern, or makes it a lot better, depending on your point of view at the moment.

Years ago, I taught some of these techniques to a friend, and he told me an interesting story about how he worked with the blue ray. He told me of a young friend of his who constantly expressed in the lust area, and of an experience they had together. They were walking down the street and the young man saw a beautiful girl, nudged my friend, and said, "Wow! Did you see that?"

He said, "Yes," and a little while later, another pretty girl passed. The young man nudged him again and said, "Wow, did you see that? "

He nodded, and a little bit further down the street they saw another lovely girl walking by, and the young man said, "Wow! Look at that!" This went on for so long that my friend decided that either this young man had to change his approach, or they would have to go their separate ways. He suggested to his young friend that there was a lot more to women than could be seen with the physical eyes and it might be nice if he tried to get his mind off sex for awhile. The young man said, "I'll do better with this."

My friend asked, "Would you mind if I helped?"

He said, "No, go ahead."

My friend asked for the master of the blue ray to be present with the boy for the highest good, and surround him. He watched as the blue Light came all around the young man and with conscious direction, he kept the blue Light swirling and moving and dynamic. He kept it activated and did not allow it to dissipate. They walked for blocks without one, "Wow, did you see that?" And when they got home, the young man didn't even reach for the first "girlie" magazine he saw—which was usually his prime evidence that the world was still the world.

About three days later, the young man contacted my friend and said, "What did you do that curtailed the lust pattern with me?"

My friend told him, "I just assisted you in the direction you said you wanted to go."

The young man said, "Well, could you sort of let go of that now?"

My friend said, "Yes, of course, it can be let go. I'm not holding it to you. If you wish to do something else, you have a right to do that." He had used the blue Light to assist the young man in his expression, not to control him. The blue ray can be very effective in helping you to control your own energy patterns and allowing you to express in the way that is for your highest good.

I also know a couple who are both "lookers." They're not lusters, just lookers. They see somebody go by, and they look. But each one suspects that the other one is lusting, and this creates a problem. Each one is thinking, "Why are you looking at that person when I'm here with you?" The answer is, "I'm just looking. It's harmless to look." But the pattern was disturbing them both, so they asked me if something could be done. I told them how they could use the blue Light. They both wanted to try it, and agreed with each asking for the blue Light for the other.

They were willing to experiment with this technique and see if they liked the results. When the woman called the blue Light in around her husband, he became the model husband. But we all know that a model is just a replica of the real thing; she felt there was no more adventure in their relationship. He wasn't looking anywhere. It was as if he was wearing blinders when they were out and about. So she explained to him what was happening. He said he hadn't even realized he wasn't looking; his mind was just on other things.

They both use this blue Light when they feel that the other's looking is becoming an irritation. If the person who is looking is looking too much, the other one sends the blue Light and cools out that activity. Because of their agreement to work this way with each other, they stayed out of the area of physic control, and had a good time exploring the technique and finding out more of what they wanted with each other. If you do this technique with another person, be sure to have their permission. Keep in mind that this is an action of psychic control. If you go into this without the knowledge and permission of the other person, it can come back on top of you. If the other person knows what you're doing and it's okay with them, then it's clear. Remember that you can't exercise control over someone else and walk away free. Use these techniques with caution, especially if you involve another person. When you ask for the highest good, and have permission from anyone else involved, you may alleviate distractions and create greater peace and calm in and around you.

Meditations

1. If you are feeling angry or upset or in emotional turmoil of some kind, ask that the master of the blue ray be present with you and release to you the power of the blue Light for the highest good. Feel yourself surrounded by the coolness of the blue ray and breathe that color into your body. Feel it move through the body and out to every extremity. Feel the blue and the coolness surround the head area and bring calmness and serenity.

2. Imagine yourself on the beach in soft, blue moonlight. Everything is suffused with soft blue. The moon overhead looks pale blue, the sky looks deep blue. The sand feels cool and as you lie there, you let the blue of the waves gently wash over you, engulfing and cleansing you. Feel the blue of the waves wash away all your disturbance, anxiety, and despair. Feel the Spirit surrounding you and filling you with peace and with a joyous love for all things.

3. Use the blue color ray in any daily situation where you are getting "too hot"—either through anger or frustration or heavy emotional involvement of any kind. Feel yourself taking off a garment of red and putting on a robe of blue. Feel the blue soft and cool against your skin. See yourself standing in the blue robe against a blue sky. Feel your oneness with all the universe, and let go of your personal point of view. Let go and become one with all things.

Purple

The master of the purple ray ushers this ray into the physical, psychic dimensions from the higher realms of Light. This is the color that the Mystical Traveler works through as it works with you. This is the highest color vibration that you can see and know and be aware of in the negative realms of Light. The Mystical Traveler works on this ray because it is a transmuter, a changer. When you ask for assistance from the Mystical Traveler and things change seemingly instantly, it's because there is a transmuting quality inherent in the Traveler Consciousness. When you see the presence of the Traveler appearing from Spirit, it often comes as a purple flash or a purple dot. There may be a little blue or gold present also, depending on the action that is being fulfilled. The colors that appear around the purple may clue you in as to what else is happening.

Purple is a transmuter. Many people who use the color purple pull it from the ground up through the body and out through the top of the head, transmuting everything in the body. This action works in the metaphysical, psychic worlds, which may be fine, but it is not working with the highest quality of consciousness available.

In MSIA, we teach bringing the purple ray of Light from the top of the head down, bringing it from the higher realms down to this physical realm of consciousness. We bring it into the body from above and down into the earth so that the negative frequencies are moved down and away from your higher spiritual centers. Then the negative frequencies are sent into the inner transmuter of the earth and dispersed.

People have asked why the Mystical Traveler doesn't manifest on the pure "white" Light. The reason is that you can't see the white Light; it's clear and cannot be seen. And you should be aware of the presence of the Traveler when there is spiritual work going on. Even more important than seeing the purple Light is *feeling* the energy of it as it comes in— the feeling of calmness or joy.

Purple has been chosen as the color of the Traveler because it is a transmuter. Blue has been chosen because of its spiritual quality. These colors represent the line of the Travelers, the school of their consciousness. Everyone who moves into MSIA as a student becomes heir to that line of energy. It brings forth all things new. It makes all things new. It changes what has been into what will be; it alters the structure of the old and brings in new patterns of growth and possibility. It awakens each one it touches to the divine heritage of the Christ Consciousness.

Meditations

1. Ask for the presence of the Mystical Traveler and the master of the purple ray for the highest good. Sense that color surround you and fill you. As you breathe it in from the top of your head, sense it transmute all things that have been negative or of the lower nature into Spirit, into Light. Sense the purple ray move slowly down through your body, moving

ahead of it all things negative, leaving behind it a feeling of pure Light and blissful awareness of Spirit. As you feel all negativity drain away through your toes, be aware that you are pure Light and allow the Traveler to release from your consciousness all things that are not for your highest good, leaving you pure.

2. Call in the Light for the highest good, close your eyes and focus your attention on the third eye area of your forehead. This is the area between and just above your eyes, back into the center of your head. Feel the energy begin to build in that area until it becomes a pulsating, tingling, alive energy. It may start rocking you a little bit. Go with whatever the action is. Then envision in your creative imagination a purple jewel, an amethyst, and place that jewel in the center of your forehead. Observe all things through that jewel. Observe all things as transmuted through the color purple.

3. For this exercise, you will need something purple. You can use a piece of construction paper, a piece of clothing, a flower, or any object that is a deep, pure purple. Place the purple item at approximately eye level or a little below, call in the Light for the highest good, and gaze at the color for several minutes. Then close your eyes and observe what happens on the inner screen of your vision. You may want to track your experiences in your journal. Repeat this exercise as often as you wish.

White

When we take all of the colors of Light—red, orange, yellow, green, blue, and purple—and combine them together in appropriate quantities, we get a white Light. This is the white Light that we refer to as the magnetic Light, the lower Light. It can't be seen, but it can be felt. There is power with it. When we work to attune ourselves to the Holy Spirit, which can manifest on the white Light ray, its presence can also be known; however, the Holy Spirit is a clear Light.

Unless the Holy Spirit is working through the Magnetic Light, you cannot tell that it is present because it is pure. When the Mystical Traveler in higher consciousness says to you, "I am always with you," that presence is with you as a clear Light, until there is an action of transmutation instituted on a lower level. Then when something happens that involves the full force of the Traveler working with you, you will see a flash of purple go across the room or up the side of a wall or down and around the floor, or come in as little dots of purple Light that dance in front of you. When people in MSIA see this, they often just say, "Hi, Traveler, I'm glad you're here." The Light and the feeling of energy are there for you to identify.

Meditations:

1. As you go about your day, ask for the white Light to surround, fill and protect you any time you think of it. Notice any changes this creates in and around you.

2. When you see someone who is disturbed or having difficulty, ask that the White Light go to them for the highest good. Perhaps you're in a grocery store and a mother is having problems with her child. Or someone in the office is having a bad day. Or a friend has lost a loved one. You can even send this white Light to people and situations in the paper or in the news on TV. There is no such thing as too much of this white Light on this planet, as long as you always ask for the highest good.

3. Whenever you are in a disturbing situation, ask for the white Light to surround, protect and fill you. Negative frequencies are dissolved by this Light, so take note of any shifts in and around you. (Of course, if you are in physical danger in any way, you would also move physically to get yourself out of any potentially harmful situations.)

4. Whenever you think of it, ask for a column of white Light to be placed wherever you are. This anchors a beautiful energy into the area for anyone else who comes that way. Busy places like shopping malls, supermarkets, concerts, movies, etc. can benefit from the uplifting quality of this Light.

14
In Conclusion

The tradition of the color rays is important to know. I suggest that you experiment with these rays and track your experiences in your journal, which will become a workbook for you as well as a record of your results. I'm sure it's all right with the masters of each ray if you ask for their assistance in your color work. Remember the concept of "the highest good." It's your protection against misusing the powers that you are working with. Whenever you work with the masters of the color rays, place the action into the Light of the Holy Spirit for the highest good.

Sometimes it may seem as if nothing takes place, and even then, accept that as for your highest good at that time. If something does take place, go with it, observe it, learn from it. On some level within you, you will be able to find a working arrangement to bring forward an understanding of this information. Maybe it's contentment, maybe it's physical balance, maybe it's joy. I tell people, "If it works for you, use it."

You check the information out by doing it, working it and tracking your experience. You become the master of your own experience, and the knowledge that you gain cannot be taken from you. If you use this information, you will find out that it does work, but only if you work it, only if you do it.

⊹ ⊹ ⊹

Glossary

astral realm. The psychic, material realm above the physical. The realm of the imagination. Intertwines with the physical as a vibratory rate.

akashic records. The karmic records, kept in the causal realm. The angel "Akasha" is the keeper of these records. Magnificent beyond comprehension, he stands in the causal realm and is aware of and knows everything that goes on within the lower realms of Light. His job is bookkeeping—a person's karma is recorded in the Akashic records.

aura. The electromagnetic energy field that surrounds the human body. Has color and movement.

basic self. One of three selves that make up physical consciousness. Has responsibility for bodily functions, maintains habits and the psychic centers of the physical body. Also known as the lower self. Handles communication from the conscious self, the self reading this, to the high self, which functions as the spiritual guardian, directing the conscious self toward spiritual progression.

causal realm. The psychic, material realm above the astral realm and below the mental realms. Intertwines somewhat with the physical realm as a vibratory rate.

cosmic mirror. The mirror at the top of the void, which is at the top of the etheric realm, just below the Soul realm. Everything that has not been cleared in the physical, astral, causal, and mental levels is projected onto the cosmic mirror.

etheric realm. The psychic, material realm above the mental realm and below the Soul realm. Equated with the unconscious or subconscious level. Sometimes known as the esoteric realm.

incarnation. We incarnate on the planet only once, and then we reembody many times, returning with a different body to gain experience, to learn, and to balance karma. Reincarnation is the popular cultural term for incarnation and reembodiment.

initiation. In MSIA, the process of being connected to the Sound Current of God.

inner realms. The astral, causal, mental, etheric, and Soul realms that exist within a person's consciousness. *see also* **outer realms.**

karma. The law of cause and effect: as you sow, so shall you reap. The responsibility of each person for his or her actions. The law that directs and sometimes dominates a being's physical existence.

Light. The energy of Spirit that pervades all realms of existence. Also refers to the Light of the Holy Spirit.

magnetic Light. The Light of God that functions in the negative realms.

mental realm. The psychic, material realm above the causal realm and below the etheric realm. Relates to the universal mind.

Movement of Spiritual Inner Awareness (MSIA). An organization whose major focus is to bring people into an awareness of Soul Transcendence. John-Roger is the founder.

Mystical Traveler Consciousness. An energy from the highest source of Light and Sound whose work on this planet is Soul Transcendence and awakening people to an awareness of the Soul. This consciousness is always anchored on the planet through a physical form.

negative realms. *See* **psychic, material realms.**

Ocean of Love and Mercy. Another term for Spirit on the Soul level and above.

outer realms. The astral, causal, mental, etheric, and Soul realms above the Soul realm also exist outside a person's consciousness, but in a greater way. *see also* **inner realms.**

physical realm. The earth. The psychic, material realm in which a being lives in a physical body.

positive realms. The Soul realm and the twenty-seven levels above the Soul realm. *see also* **psychic, material realms.**

psychic. Nonphysical, and frequently invisible, but below the Soul realm.

psychic, material realms. The five lower, negative realms; namely, the physical, astral, causal, mental, and etheric realms. *see also* **positive realms.**

realms. *see* **inner realms and outer realms.**

s.e.'s. *see* **spiritual exercises.**

Soul. The extension of God individualized within each human being. The basic element of human existence, forever connected to God. The God within.

Soul realm. The realm above the etheric realm. The first of the positive realms and the true home of the Soul. The first level where the Soul is consciously aware of its true nature, its pure beingness, its oneness with God.

Soul Transcendence. To transcend the lower levels (physical, astral, causal, mental, and etheric) and move into the Soul realm and above. The work of the Mystical Traveler.

Soul travel. Moving the consciousness into the Soul body and then traveling in the Soul body to realms of consciousness other than the physical realm. Sometimes known as out-of-body experiences. This can be done on one's own inner realms or in the outer realms, the higher spiritual realms. (This is different from astral travel, in which the consciousness leaves the body and travels in the astral realm. MSIA does not teach astral travel or astral projection.) *see also* inner realms and outer realms.

Sound Current. The audible energy that flows from God through all realms. The spiritual energy on which a person returns to the heart of God.

Spirit. The essence of creation. Infinite and eternal.

spiritual exercises (s.e.'s). Chanting the HU, the Ani-Hu, or one's initiatory tone. An active technique of bypassing the mind and emotions by using a spiritual tone to connect to the Sound Current. Assists a person in breaking through the illusions of the lower levels and eventually moving into an awareness of the Soul consciousness and above.

universal mind. Located at the highest part of the etheric realm, at the division between the negative and positive realms. Gets its energy from the mental realm. The source of the individual mind.

⊕⊕⊕

Bibliography of
Books & Tapes by John-Roger

Items are audio tapes unless otherwise noted. V preceding a number denotes the tape is also available in video format. SAT stands for Soul Awareness Tapes, which are audio tapes of J-R seminars, meditations, and sharings that are sent each month only to SAT subscribers. Once you subscribe, you can obtain previously issued tapes.

BREATHING MEDITATIONS

Joyful Meditations Volume 1 (#3700)
    especially "The Breathing Meditation"

Soul Journey through Spiritual Exercises
    (Three tape album, with booklet; #3718)
    especially "H-U Chant" & "Breathing Meditation"

CHANTS - ANI-HU Chant

"Ani-Hu" (#1610)

"Chanting the Sacred Tones"
    (#7001, Spanish/English)

"The Law of Empathy" (#3004)

Spiritual Exercises: Walking with the Lord
    (Four tape album, #3907)
    especially "Medley 2" on "Spiritual Exercise
    Medleys"

CHANTS - HU Chant

"The HU Meditation" (#1800)

"Chanting the Sacred Tones"
(#7001, Spanish/English)

"Luxor Meditation for Peace and Harmony"
PAT IV, Volume 7 (#7303)

Soul Journey through Spiritual Exercises
(Three tape album, with booklet; #3718)
especially "H-U Chant" & "Breathing Meditation"

Spiritual Exercises: Walking with the Lord
(Four tape album, #3907)
especially "Medley 1" on "Spiritual Exercise
Medleys"

CHANTS - So-Hawng Chant

Joyful Meditations Volume II (#3705)
especially "The So-Hawng Meditation"

LIGHT- Magnetic Light, Spiritual Light,
White Light

"A Matter of Degrees" (#7190, SAT tape)

"How Can You Tell the Level of Light in You?"
(#7296, SAT tape)

HU-Man...God Man (#7328, SAT tape)

LIGHT- Magnetic Light, Spiritual Light,
White Light (continued)

Joyful Meditations Volume 1 (#3700)
especially "The White Light Meditation"

"The Suffering of Man, His Dilemma, and the
White Light Meditation" (#2591)

REALMS OF LIGHT

"Inner Journey Through Spirit Realms" (#7251)

"Passages to the Realms of Spirit" (#7037, #V-7037)

"Sights and Sounds on the Inner Journey" (#2128)

"Sounds of the Realms" (#2530)

"Where are the Worlds Without End?" (#V-7125)

SPIRITUAL EXERCISES

"Basic Instructions for Spiritual Exercises"
(#7535, SAT tape)

"Simran - Chanting the Sacred Tones" (#2538)

Soul Journey through Spiritual Exercises
(Three tape album, with booklet; #3718)
"Seminar: Human Spiritual Rights"
"H-U Chant & Breathing Meditation"
"Meditation for Soul Travel"

SPIRITUAL EXERCISES *(continued)*

Spiritual Exercises: From Distraction to Divine Experience (Two tape album, with booklet; #3810)

"Spiritual Exercises and Question & Answers with John-Roger"

"Spiritual Exercises Innerphasing and Spiritual Exercises Affirmations "

Spiritual Exercises: Walking with the Lord (Four tape album, #3907)

"25 Years of S.E. Excerpts" (1968-1992)

"What's the Value of Doing Spiritual Exercises? and Useful Keys for S.E.'S"

"Spiritual Exercise Medleys"

"Keys and Blocks to Soul Transcendence"

Spiritual Exercises: Walking with the Lord (Three tape album, #3908)

"Mantra & Prayers"

"Divine Imagination: A Key to Higher Consciousness"

"Simran - Chanting the Sacred Tones"

Walking with the Lord (Book, #930-0)

OTHER - Meditation Albums, Guided Meditations

"A Walk in the Forest" (#3716)

OTHER - Meditation Albums, Guided Meditations
(*continued*)

Joyful Meditations Volume 1 (#3700)
"The Breathing Meditation"
"The Inner Calm"
"The Golden Temple Meditation"
"The White Light Meditation"

Joyful Meditations Volume II (#3705)
"The Light Attunement"
"The Meditation of Understanding"
"The Meditation of Perfect Balance"
"The So-Hawng Meditation"

Joyful Meditations Volume III (#3710)
"The Meditation of the Christ"
"The Meditation of Forgiveness"
"Sara's Meditation"
"The Meditation of Objectivity"

"Practicing the Divine Presence" (#3715)

OTHER - Ongoing Spiritual Study

Soul Awareness Discourses
If you liked this book, Discourses are a gold mine
of further information.(12 books per year, one for
each month, English, Spanish, or French, #5000)

Soul Awareness Tape (SAT) Series
A new John-Roger seminar every month, plus access to the entire SAT library of hundreds of meditations & seminars. (12 tapes per year, one sent each month, #5400)

Dream Voyages (Book, #931-9)
Forgiveness, The Key to the Kingdom (Book, #934-3)
Manual on Using the Light (Book, #913-0)
The Path to Mastership (Book, #916-5)
The Power Within You (Book, #924-6)
The Tao of Spirit (Book, #933-5)

RELAXING THE BODY

"Being Your Own Creator" (#7315, SAT tape)

"Relax and Love Yourself Healthy" (#7182)

"Psychic Reintegration and Body Relaxation" (#3717)

Tapes and books are available from:

MSIA®
PO Box 513935
Los Angeles, CA 90051
213-737-4055
soul@msia.org
http://www.msia.org

About the Author

Since 1963, John-Roger has traveled all over the world, lecturing, teaching, and assisting people who want to create a life of greater health, happiness, peace, and prosperity and a greater awakening to the Spirit within. His humor and practical wisdom have benefited thousands and lightened many a heart.

In the course of this work, he has given over 4,000 seminars, many of which are televised nationally on "That Which Is." He has also written more than 30 books, including 2 *New York Times* bestsellers.

The common thread throughout all John-Roger's work is loving, opening to the highest good of all, and the awareness that God is abundantly present and available.

If you've enjoyed this book, you may want to explore and delve more deeply into what John-Roger has shared about this subject and other related topics. See the bibliography for a selection of study materials. For an even wider selection of study materials and more information on John-Roger's teachings through MSIA, please contact us at:

MSIA®
P.O. Box 513935
Los Angeles, CA 90051-1935
(213) 737-4055
soul@msia.org
http://www.msia.org